Newber

Newberry Volcano is the largest ice-age volcano, by volume, in the Northwest.

The Big Obsidian Flow, at 1,350 years of age, is the youngest lava flow in Oregon.

Hot springs bubble up in both East and Paulina Lakes.

Newberry's geological diversity is unsurpassed by any other volcanic landform in the United States.

The first Euro-American to record a visit to Newberry was Peter Skene Ogden, of the Hudson's Bay Company, when he explored the area in 1826.

The volcano is named for Dr. John Strong Newberry, who traveled through the area as a member of the Pacific Railroad Survey in 1855.

The Oregon Pumice Grapefern is a rare plant that is found at Newberry and at only two other sites in the world — both also in Oregon. It is awaiting listing on the Federal Endangered Species list.

Bald eagles and other endangered species are found here.

The world's record brown trout was caught in Paulina Lake.

An unbelievably rich series of Native American sites are present in the Monument area and are available for interpretation.

The "ecosystem approach" to protection has included plant communities from the riparian areas along the Deschutes River to the subalpine ones at Paulina Peak.

A magma source (or sources) is possibly located several kilometers beneath the volcano.

The geothermal energy resource, as estimated by the Bonneville Power Administration, is about 1,500 to 2,000 megawatts. This is greater than   Bonneville Dam or Trojan Nuclear Plant.

NEWBERRY
NATIONAL VOLCANIC
MONUMENT

America's Newest National Monument

AN OREGON DOCUMENTARY

Stuart G. Garrett

Bert Webber, Editor

WEBB RESEARCH GROUP

Direct all inquiries to the Publisher:
WEBB RESEARCH GROUP PUBLISHERS
P. O. Box 314
Medford, OR 97501

Cover Illustrations
Front cover: (TOP) Paulina Peak (Bert Webber)
(LOWER) Pauline Lake–left; East Lake–right
(Webber collection)
(INSET) Oregon's largest brown trout 27 lbs. 12 oz.
(John Hofferd collection)
Back cover: Paulina Falls (Margie Webber)

NOTE: The Newberry National Volcanic Monument, being a federal property, collects a "Day Use" fee. Guests of Paulina Lake Lodge and East Lake Resort are exempt from paying this fee. However, if guests of these facilities otherwise use the national monument, as climbing Paulina Peak, etc., then the fee will be collected. The terms of the fee schedule may change without notice.

Depending on snow and road conditions, the lakes and lodges are usually open for the beginning of the High Lakes fishing season late in April and remain open through October. Paulina Lake Lodge operates a Winter Season from mid-December through mid-March. Dates of operations may change without notice.

Library of Congress Cataloging-in-Publication Data

Garrett, Stuart G., 1950-
    Newberry National Volcanic Monument ; an Oregon
documentary / Stuart G. Garrett ; Bert Webber, editor.
      p.   cm.
    Includes biographical references and index
    ISBN 0-936738-46-4
    1. Newberry National Volcanic Monument (Or.)—Guide books.
I. Webber, Bert. II Title.
F882.DrG37   1991   91-13081
917.95'87—dc20   CIP

Table of Contents

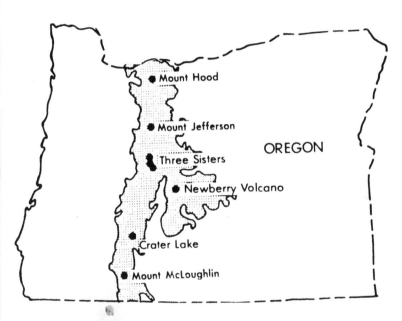

Major volcanic centers and areas of Quaternary volcanic
rocks in Oregon. (From ORE. GEOLOGY Vol.44 No. 11,
Nov. 1982.)

(Opposite page) This pre-1920 view shows the road south of Bend
near the National Monument. These low-elevation ponderosa pine
trees were clear-cut in the original timber harvests after 1916. The
lack of undergrowth is due to frequent fires which would clear the
forest floor.

NEWBERRY TIMELINE

 640 - Big Obsidian Flow erupts, forming largest such flow in the Northwest and Oregon's youngest lava flow.

1826 - Peter Skene Ogden records first Euro-American visit to Newberry caldera while trapping for the Hudson's Bay Company.

1855 - Dr. John Strong Newberry travels volcano's flanks while accompanying the Pacific Railroad Survey under leadership of Lts. Williamson and Abbot, U.S. Army Corps of Topographical Engineers.

1904 - Crater Lake designated Oregon's first National Park. Newberry was also considered.

1911 - First fish transplanted to caldera's lakes.

1920 - Professor Crosby recommends park status for Newberry.

1921 - Newberry examined at request of Bend Commercial Club for National Park designation.

1937 - NPS surveys Newberry for special designation.

1940 - Editorial in Bend *Bulletin* and consulting geologist support park designation.

1943 - Salem Chemetekens and Federation of Western Outdoor Clubs propose National Park.

1976 - Newberry designated National Natural Landmark by NPS; KGRA (Known Geothermal Resource Area) formed and leases purchased.

1977 - Conservationists propose Park to stop geothermal exploration.

1981 - USGS geothermal test well hits 509°F at 3,058 ft.

1984 - Stosh Thompson proposes idea of 120,000 acre park but finds little support.

1987 - Newberry Volcano National Monument committee formed.

1989 - (Feb.) Marathon boundary meeting accomplished.

1989 - (Nov.) Newberry Monument legislation introduced in Congress.

1990 - (Oct.) Bill passed by U.S. House and Senate.

1990 - (Nov.) Bill signed by President George Bush.

Introduction

In many ways, this book and this monument have been over 50 years in the making. Newberry Volcano, the Deschutes River, the various lava features and East and Paulina Lakes, have long been recognized as special areas. This recognition began with the Native Americans and has persisted down through the various inhabitants of Central Oregon.

Today, sightseers can travel to the summit of Paulina Peak to enjoy magnificent vistas. Skiers and snowmobilers enjoy winter sports all over the volcano. During the fishing season, fishermen are found constantly on the lakes in the caldera and recreationists of all sorts enjoy this wonderful area.

The recognition that has been extended to Newberry Volcano is well deserved. It is a mountain of superlatives. It is the largest volcano by volume in the Pacific Northwest. Its sheer size dwarfs most of the better known volcanic peaks in the Cascade Range to the west. The Monument contains Oregon's youngest lava flow — the Big Obsidian Flow that oozed from the ground a mere 1,350 years ago. It is the largest of several obsidian flows in central Oregon.

The National Monument includes an extremely diverse group of volcanic eruptions. Low-silica basaltic lavas, accompanied by cinder cones and a complex of underground lava tubes and caves, are found at lower elevations on the volcano.

The caldera itself is a geologic wonderland. Rhyolitic and obsidian flows are found there in addition to pumice cones and maar volcanos. Each of these are discussed in this book.

The Newberry National Volcanic Monument is unique in Oregon in that it includes a broad swath of plant communities. These communities begin with the riparian systems found along the banks of the Deschutes River which merge with the ponderosa pine and lodgepole pine forests found at higher elevations. As one ascends higher on the volcanic flanks, a zone of mixed conifers is encountered. Finally, these plants give way to the sub-alpine, windswept, white-bark pines along the caldera rim.

Wildlife abounds within the monument. On any given day a bald eagle may be seen soaring above the lakes in its search for food. Black bears occasionally are reported in the more remote parts of the caldera. Elk and deer are at home in these woods. During the summers, a variety of waterfowl frequent the lakes. A wide number of birds are found throughout the lower elevation forests.

Little did Dr. John Strong Newberry, geologist, know that one hundred and thirty-five years after he traversed the lower flanks of this volcano, it would be named for him. As the scientist with the Williamson-Abbot expedition, he explored the lower reaches of the volcano.* Newberry later went on to academic geology and one of his students, Israel C. Russell, named the feature for his respected teacher.

This book is meant to serve as a general introduction to the history, natural features, and the many interesting aspects of Newberry Volcano and the Newberry National Volcanic Monument. It is meant to be accurate, easy to use, and easy to understand. For the reader wishing more details, I would refer him to the excellent references in the bibliography. This is a well studied and reasonably well understood volcano and much more technical detail is available.

*   *   *

This book is the result of a long-standing love affair with Newberry Volcano. My interest has, over the years, led me to pursue various facets of natural history associated with this volcano. These chapters are, in great part, a result of those investigations. However, I had excellent help writing this book and I'd like to recognize those who assisted.

Bruce Nolf, Ph.D., a superb geology instructor at Central Oregon Community College in Bend, is responsible for kindling my early geologic interest in Newberry. Accompanying him on course-associated field trips awakened my appreciation for this little-known wonder. Bob Jensen contributed substantially to the chapters on geology. His book, *Roadside Guide to the Geology of Newberry Volcano,* is a remarkable compilation of geologic knowledge and is indispensable to those interested in Newberry's geologic history. He has kindly reviewed, updated, and partially rewritten the geologic information in this work. Larry Chitwood, geologist with the Deschutes National Forest, has worked on the volcano for a long time and has contributed heavily to my understanding of it.

Bill Hopkins, Ph.D., is a botanist and ecologist for the Forest

---

*Dr. Newberry was a member of a U.S. Army Corps of Topographical Engineers expedition to determine a suitable route between the Sacramento River and the Columbia River for a railroad. The very large scientific party and its armed escort, as protection from Indians, was commanded by Lieutenant Robert W. Williamson, U.S.A. On the trek northbound, the party generally followed the Deschutes River but took many side trips. One of these variations in route was led by Dr. Newberry. Lieutenant Henry L. Abbot, mentioned, was second in command of this expedition.

Service. I have spent many hours hiking the flanks of Newberry with him. Always appreciative of his botanical enthusiasm and humor, I am grateful for his review and comments dealing with vegetation and fire.

Russell Mitchell, Ph.D., has recently retired from the Silviculture Lab, Bend, He is a thoughtful entomologist and has advised me regarding insects and forest diseases.

Steve Matz, archaeologist for the Deschutes National Forest, has kindly reviewed my chapters on the indigenous peoples and made important comments.

Ed Park is an outdoor and travel writer/photographer in Bend. He prepared a story about the big fish from Paulina Lake that appeared in *Field & Stream* in April of 1972. He has generously allowed the use of his fascinating story of the world-record trout from Paulina Lake to be included here.

John and Leslie Hofferd, East Lake, contributed heavily about the commercial history at both Paulina and East Lake resorts.

I very much appreciate the assistance provided by numerous foresters from Fort Rock Ranger District and from Lava Lands Visitor's Center, Deschutes National Forest. These folks allowed access to their photo archives and provided the list of birds found in the area. Margie Webber, bird-watcher and editor, prepared the list for inclusion here.

Bert Webber, Editor-in-Chief and Publisher at Webb Research Group, goaded me into becoming involved with this project. His recognition of the importance of America's newest national monument and the need for a good general guide have provided the impetus for this book. He assisted greatly with preparation of the manuscript and located or took many of the photographs included here. Bert completely and competently handled layout and production of the book. His attention to detail and his desire for accuracy are evident.

I hope this book will serve to whet the appetite of visitors and will encourage them to delve deeper into the fascinating story of Newberry Volcano. I have meticulously striven for accuracy throughout and appreciate the contributions of the experts mentioned. But should there be oversights or errors, I accept full responsibility. Constructive comments are encouraged. These should be sent to me in care of the publisher.

I have arranged that any profits that are mine from the sale of this book will be donated to the Friends of Newberry National Volcanic Monument.

Stu Garrett
Bend, Oregon

Forester demonstrates arrowhead making using
obsidian.

Be it Enacted:
The Making of a Monument

From early days, Newberry has been recognized as a special area. The similarity of the five-mile-in-diameter caldera to Crater Lake, 65 air-miles to the southwest, was noticed early on. The mysteries of the caldera's geology were probed from the time of the early explorers on through today. Recreationists and nature lovers have always treasured this spot.

It was in the 1920's that the Bend Commercial Club began a campaign for special park-like designation for Newberry. Professor Crosby, a geologist from an eastern university, traveled the area. In his reports he remarked upon the geologic significance of the Lava River Cave, the lava flows associated with Newberry and the volcano itself. Nothing, however, came of his study. The idea for preserving the area as a park was resurrected again in the 1940's. But it was not until the 1970's that a strong and determined legislative attempt was made to protect Newberry.

At about this time it became evident there was probability that Newberry Volcano could be a source for geothermal energy. A group of local citizens, including Dwight and Mary Newton, sought a degree of protection for the area. As a result of their efforts and in cooperation with Senator Sam Johnson, the 1975 Oregon Legislature, under House Joint Resolution 31, directed the State Energy Facility Siting Council, to forbid thermal power plants in an almost 40,000 acre area centered on the caldera. Subsequently, the State of Oregon, Deschutes County and the U.S. Forest Service all drew boundaries on the volcano with varying degrees of allowance for development of geothermal power.

In 1976 the Department of Interior, acting through the National Park Service, designated Newberry caldera and some areas on its flanks as a National Natural Landmark. This program is a way the federal government has developed of drawing attention to preserving unique examples of natural features in our country. One commentator has observed that "these Landmarks are considered 'ladies in waiting' for park status."

In the 1980's, Stephen Thompson developed a vision of a national designation at Newberry. He drew boundary lines which linked up the Newberry caldera with special management areas along the northwest rift zone to the north of the caldera. These included the Lava Cast Forest, the Lava River Caves, and the Lava Butte Geologic Area. Thompson proceeded to approach the Forest Service, the Chamber of Commerce and anyone who would listen with his ideas but the timing was not right.

In the late 1980's, it became apparent that Newberry Volcano was destined for geothermal development. Over 40 geothermal exploratory wells had been drilled in the caldera and on the flanks of the volcano. The hottest geothermal well in the northwest was drilled at Newberry by the U.S. Geologic Survey. The temperature of 510^0 Fahrenheit was found at a depth of 3,100 feet in a well drilled in 1981 near the Big Obsidian Flow. This temperature is hotter than the temperatures at The Geysers in California, which is the world's largest geothermal field. The Bonneville Power Administration subsequently estimated the electrical generating potential at Newberry as somewhere between 1,500 and 2,000 megawatts. This would be larger than the output from either Trojan Nuclear Power Plant, Oregon's only nuclear facility, or the Bonneville Dam. Two companies, California Energy and GEO Newberry Crater, Inc., became active in geothermal leasing and exploration at Newberry. It became obvious that if a special designaion was ever to be sought for this area, the time had come.

In the fall of 1987, Stephen Thompson, Tom Throop, Paul Dewey, Don Tryon, and Stu Garrett met to discuss the situation. A decision was reached at that meeting to seek a solution to the concern for development versus conservation at Newberry.

It was decided at this meeting that the group would seek a special, national designation for a portion of Newberry Volcano. The group hoped to accomplish this by establishing a Consensus Committee to develop a proposal. Members of all potential interest-groups were invited to take part in the process. There were representatives of conservation groups, the geothermal industry, timber industry, skiiers, snowmobilers, hunters and fishermen, as well as people from various governmental agencies. It was determined that it would take a series of meetings in order to identify all the issues and concerns. By February 1989, the Consensus Committee was ready to draw a proposed boundary. This critical meeting, at which this was accomplished, went from 1:00 in the afternoon to 1:00 the next morning. During this 12-hour marathon, the group was able to draw the boundaries of the Monument as well as agree on a series of management guidelines that helped to outline the proposal. With papers in hand and a strong body of business, civic leaders and a large band of local citizens agreeing, the group approached Congressman Bob Smith within whose district the entire Monument proposal lies. He eagerly volunteered his support for the plan. Through his office, a bill was drafted and introduced in Congress in November 1989.

At this point legislative lobbying began. Central Oregon citizens pushed hard for support. In Washington D.C., offices of conservation, industry, as well as other groups, made their opinions known about the proposal. It was within the U.S. House of Representatives where most of the negotiation and deliberation took place. In June 1990, the National Parks and Public Lands subcommittee of the House Interior Committee held a key hearing on the Bill. Representative Bob Smith guided the Bill through the maze of legislative processes. The subcommittee chairman, Representative Bruce Vento, Minnesota, made a field trip to the Monument in July to see firsthand what proponents were talking about. Further work on the Bill continued well into October then the House unanimously passed the Bill in October. Under the guidance of Senator Mark Hatfield, the Senate also passed the Bill. President George Bush signed the Newberry National Volcanic Monument into law on November 5, 1990 and America's newest National Monument was born. The formal dedication was on June 30, 1991 at Lava Lands Visitor's Center, on Highway 97, in the Monument. □

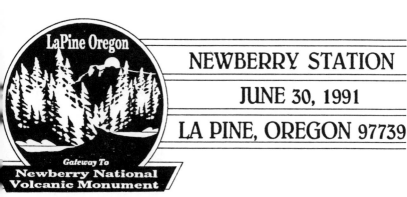

LaPine Oregon

NEWBERRY STATION

JUNE 30, 1991

LA PINE, OREGON 97739

Gateway To
Newberry National Volcanic Monument

The United States Postal Service issued a commemorative postmark on June 30, 1991, Dedication Day for Newberry National Volcanic Monument. The special post office, ''Newberry Station,'' operated only on that day from a temporary post office set up within the Monument. See page 121. The nearest regular post office is in nearby La Pine.

Cultural History

The first inhabitants of Central Oregon are presumed to have crossed the Bering land bridge from Siberia into Alaska then moved southward into western North America. Scientists disagree among themselves as to when this migration took place, but practically all anthropologists agree that this invasion had occurred by about 10,000 years ago, but some feel there is evidence that this relocation may have occurred as early as 15,000 to 20,000 years ago.

Current archeologic and anthrpologic research will eventually answer this question. Some of the strong evidence for early occupation of western North America was gathered not far from Newberry in the Fort Rock basin.

Dr. Luther S. Cressman, Ph.D., of the University of Oregon, excavated archaeological sites in the basin in the 1930's and later. In a rock shelter not far from Fort Rock, he uncovered evidence of ancient habitation. It was while on one of these field trips that he discovered, among other artifacts, a number of sagebrush bark woven sandals which have been dated to 13,000 radiocarbon years before the present time. (Note: Radiocarbon and calendar years are not the same.)

At the time the sandal-makers lived in the Fort Rock area, there was undoubtedly a large body of water present. This water was the remnant of the vast Pleistocene lake that filled the basin to a depth of hundreds of feet. This lake was surrounded by marshes which teemed with waterfowl and fresh water fish. In fact, fossil salmon bones can still be located in the drifting sand dunes of the basin. These bones indicate that at one time there was a connection of this now-closed-in-basin with a river that emptied eventually into the ocean. In all likelihood, the numerous lava flows on the southern flanks of Newberry Volcano could have blocked off this ancient route to the sea.

Evidence of the early native American inhabitants is found throughout Fort Rock basin. These people hunted waterfowl, rabbit, deer, antelope and other animals with bow and arrows and *atalatl*. The *atalatl* was a short stick that had greater range than a spear. Many of the dart and arrow points were made from obsidian which was obtained at quarries in the Newberry caldera. To the west of the volcano, near the Deschutes River, there was a well-known and well-used travel corridor. The fluid basaltic lavas funneled travelers through an area which saw traffic by native Americans, explorers and later stockmen, ranchers, lumbermen, homesteaders and eventually became the route for Highway 97.

Rock shelters, such as the Lava Island Rock Shelter along the Deschutes River, have yielded more information about ancient local people. An excavation of the Lava Island Rock Shelter by Rick Minor and Kathryn Toepel in the 1970's revealed some fascinating information about these early inhabitants. The researchers recovered over 8,000 pieces of chipped stone in and near the shelter. By examining the trace elements present in the obsidian, they were able to determine that the majority of the obsidian came from nearby Newberry caldera. Some obsidian also came from as far away as Beatty's Butte in eastern Oregon and other spots in the western Cascades.

The bones and plant remains found within the shelter indicated that the shelter was used primarily as a hunting camp. Deer bones were very common, but other animal species were also present. The native Americans, apparently, had also used fresh water mollusks from the Deschutes River as well as fish. The larger obsidian points found here were similar to styles found along the Columbia River, but the smaller arrowheads were comparable to the Great Basin styles. These archaeologists felt that the most recent occupants of the rock shelter were probably Northern Paiute. Samples of charcoal were analyzed to give radiocarbon dates. The earliest date was determined to be 200 years B.C. There was also evidence that a bark-lined storage pit had been present as well as a cache of projectile points was found. The types of points found at the shelter would suggest that the time of occupation was from 5,000 B.C. to 8,600 B.C.

In the process of excavating the rock shelter, over 4,000 plant seeds and seed fragments were recovered. They revealed much about the use of plants by Native Americans. The seeds of ponderosa pine *(Pinus ponderosa)* were the most frequent. These had been collected by the native people and these seeds were either eaten raw or roasted. Couture points out the manner in which the Indians would use these seeds.

> Pine cones were gathered from the base of the trees and from creek beds after chipmunks and squirrels cut off the cones and dropped them. They were then taken back to camp where a large fire was built.
>
> The cones were covered with hot ashes and the pine nuts cracked and fell out. They were then winnowed, ground on metates and worked in the same manner as other seeds.

Minor and Toepel point out other uses of the Ponderosa pine tree such as use of inner bark as a sweetener and the pitch as a means

17

of waterproofing cooking baskets. The bark was used in construction of the bark-lined storage pits. The wood was a favorite of the Klamath Indians for making dugout canoes.

Other plant remains identified in the excavation were bitterbrush *(Purshia tridentata)* the seeds coats of which were used to make a dye. The berries of greenleaf manzanita *(Arctostaphylos patula)* were eaten. Buckbush *(Ceanothus velutinus)* was used as a tea. Wax currant *(Ribes cereum)* berries were found which were either eaten fresh or dried.

It is a step back in time to walk the trail along the Deschutes River to this rock shelter. The U.S. Forest Service has erected interpretive displays to point out not only the rock shelter but the native plants along the trail that were used by the aboriginal peoples. One can sit quietly on a rock at the mouth of the shelter and wonder what a native American of 10,000 years earlier must have seen.

In historic times, the Paiutes would utilize resources such as those found in this area during their annual seasonal rounds of hunting and gathering. At any particular time of year, a band of Indians would travel to wherever the food and material resources were to be found. In spring they would visit areas where they could dig roots of camas *(Camassia quamash)* and biscuit root *(Lomatium species)*.

The summer season would take them to berry fields. In the fall these people hunted antelope, deer, and there were rabbit drives. During winter season, there was fishing and hunting of waterfowl.

Each band of Paiutes took their name from the most commonly used food source. For example, Northern Paiutes who lived in the area of the present city of Bend, were called Juniper-deer eaters — Wa'dihichi'tika. This spelling varies depending on the source.

The most well-known Indian, and probably the person who has more central Oregon geographic features named for him than any other was Chief Paulina. He was shot to death in the upper reaches of Trout Creek in 1867. Paulina had been the terror of settlers for several years and had been caught in the act of stealing cattle. Howard Maupin brought him down with a single shot, then James Clark's bullets killed him. From time to time the settlers had banded and set out to track these renegades. During skirmishes between whites and Indians there were losses on both sides.

A series of cinder cones on the north side of Newberry Volcano are locally referred to as the Paulina Mountains. Paulina Peak also preserves the memory of the Chief as does the town of Paulina, Paulina Marsh, Paulina Creek, Paulina Falls, Paulina Lake, and Paulina Prairie. (The city of Maupin, Wasco County, is named for Howard Maupin.) □

The Newberry Area
in Historic Times

The Paiutes and other native Americans have long made their mark on Newberry. They knew the area well and traveled it frequently. However, the first white man to leave a record of his visit to the area was Hudson's Bay Company fur-trapper, Peter Skene Ogden

Ogden was a Quebecer who was born in 1794. He received some education in London then returned to North America where he joined the North West Company. In 1821 he became an employee of the Hudson's Bay Company when the two fur companies merged.

Ogden trapped and explored under the direction of Dr. John McLoughlin, out of Hudson's Bay Company's post at Ft. Vancouver, in what is now the state of Washington (just across the Columbia River from Portland). He was an extremely competent outdoorsman and was well respected by his superiors as well as by his hirelings. Ogden traveled with a contingent of French-Canadian trappers who frequently brought their wives and children.

It was on Ogden's 1826-27 trip that he traveled through the Newberry area. At the time he had about 35 in his party. He left Fort Vancouver, traveled up the Columbia River Gorge through the Dalles then up the Deschutes River. From there he went overland to an area near the present city of Burns, exploring the various lakes and basins as he came upon them. It was on Wednesday, November 2, that he and his party turned to the west from the Burns area and headed for the Upper Deschutes drainage. Winter was nearly upon them and it was cold at the approximately 4,000-foot elevation where they traveled. There was snow. The trip was becoming difficult. They found a number of Indians along the trail who were in extremely bad condition. Ogden states in his journal:

> An old woman who encamped with some nights since and who was very communicative and informative she gave us of the country around us I have discovered to be the most correct also informed us from the severity of the weather last year they were so extremely reduced for want of food....

During their travel across the central Oregon sagebrush country, now blowing with snow, Ogden and his party were reduced to one meal a day, noting that many of the Indians they saw were passing many days without food and still "without a complaint or a mur-

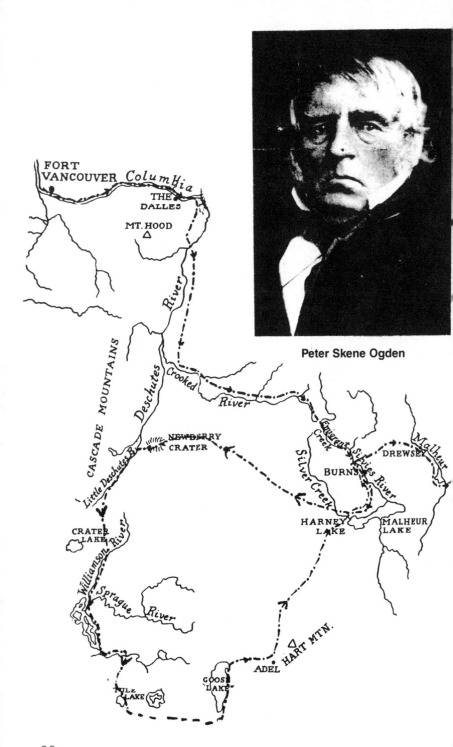

Peter Skene Ogden

mur in this wretched manner."

On Wednesday, November 9, 1826, the party first sighted the Cascade Range, probably from the area around Hampton, in Deschutes County.

Ogden goes on:

> We did not encamp until near sunset and from the mildness of the weather this day and yesterday we had some trouble in finding snow enough to supply our wants as for our poor horses they must go without for a distance of 12 miles.

Not far from Pine Mountain, Ogden noted again:

> . . . snow scarce, our horses suffer greatly and although repeated attempts have been made by melting snow in skins to make them drink few have been induced to drink.

Shortly afterwards, hunters saw four Indians. They were shy and refused to return to the camp with the hunters.

On Tuesday, the 14th, Ogden recorded:

> Our poor horses who not only require water but food and also rest and we stand certainly in need of food for within the last 10 days we have had only 6 meals and these slight ones. This is really a wretched country and certainly no other inducement but *filthy Lucre* can induce an honest man to visit it and after all his prospects of obtaining it are most gloomy. It is now 3 months since we started and only yet 500 beavers and the winter is on eve on commencing.

The party tried to rest themselves and the horses until the 16th, Wednesday, when they broke camp. Ogden:

> On starting we commenced ascending and continued so for 2 hours in strong wood covered with falling trees which caused considerable trouble to pass over with loaded horses. We there reached what I supposed to be the height of land. We then descended and at the foot of the hill, we had the pleasure of finding two lakes. One small and the other from appearances appears to be a large body of water. But we must wait for clear weather to ascertain its length and width, in our present unfortunate situation we may certainly consider these lakes as godsends. It was certainly a consolation to me if not to all to see our poor horses quench their thurst.
>
> On the height of land we had a foot of snow but here we have none nor do we require any, we are still surrounded by strong woods and it is certainly strange to find lakes at the foot of a high mountain. This gives hopes they must discharge in some river probably not far from us. God grant it.

Norway pines and a few hemlocks were the only two kinds of wood we saw in our travels this day. A number of bear tracks seen and all our riflemen in pursuit. This is the season bears serch winter lodgings and are all well loaded with fat and a dozen of them would be most exceptable to us and surely we stand in need if ever mortals did. Our hunters returned late in the evening without success. Starve we must. Our course this day southwest — distance 10 miles. Thursday the 17th we had certainly a cold night. The ice a half an inch thickness on the lake, this morning fine and clear. The lake that appeared of a large size we had a full view of this morning and it is not more than a mile in length and one-third in width. It was 11:00 AM ere all horses were found when we started leaving the lakes to the northward of us. We had not gone far when we found it was impossible to pass and we were obliged to have recourse to our axes to cut a road. This continued for 3 miles when we again reached another lake equal in size to the one we left this morning. We proceeded on and after sunset we reached a small river, here also another lake and encamped. We had for some distance not a stony road but literally a flinty one of a very large size. Though all are ignorant of this river it must from the course it takes either discharge in the Clammett Country or near the headwaters of the river of the falls. Many of the horses although greatly fatigued all reach the encampment.

On Friday, November 18, Ogden and his party traveled down to the Deschutes River. In his diary he refers to it as the "river of the falls," as translated from his French. From this point, they traveled south up the Little Deschutes River and crossed into the Klamath drainage traveling down the Williamson River near Klamath Marsh.

So Ogden described his travels through the country. It is obvious from his notes that he came up through the Millican Valley, entered the ponderosa pine forest on the east flanks of the volcano and traveled along that side coming over the "height of land" and looking down upon East Lake from the rim of the caldera. Ogden was obviously frustrated with these travels through central Oregon. Because he was looking for beaver and there weren't any, he determined that central Oregon would be of little benefit to Hudson's Bay Company from a fur-trapping point of view.

A few years later, in 1834, trapper and entrepreneur Nathaniel J. Wyeth passed through central Oregon and also explored the upper Deschutes country. But Wyeth left no record of having visited Newberry caldera although he likely passed through the lower areas of the Monument along the Deschutes River on this expedition.

The next recorded visitation was by the famous explorer John C. Fremont on his second expedition of 1843. Fremont was freshly returned from his successful expedition of 1842 during which he explored the area that is now Wyoming. Fremont was the beneficiary of his powerful father-in-law, expansionist-Senator Thomas Hart Benton of Missouri and the senator's intelligent daughter, Jessie Benton Fremont.

Fremont set out from Independence, Missouri in 1843 as part of a wagon train. His main scout was Tom Fitzpatrick, who was assisted by Kit Carson. They traveled most of what became the Oregon Trail, passing through Idaho into the Blue Mountains of Oregon, down the Columbia River then southward up the Deschutes River drainage. The stated request from Senator Benton had been to "connect the reconnaissance of 1842 with the surveys of Commander Wilkes on the coast of the Pacific Ocean." The unstated aim of this expedition was to cement the United States claim to what are now Oregon, Washington and Idaho. Fremont's trip was also meant to serve as an exploration and mapping of what soon would be commonly called "The Oregon Trail."

As Fremont passed throughout the central Oregon area, he made these notes in his journal:

> December the 5th. Today the country was all pine forests, and beautiful weather made our journey delightful. It was too warm for winter clothes; and the snow, which lay everywhere in patches through the forest, was melting rapidly. After a few hours ride, we came upon a fine stream in the middle of the forest which proved to be the principal branch of the Fall River. It was occasionally 200 feet wide sometimes narrow to 50 feet; the water is very clear and frequently deep. We ascended along the river, which sometimes presented sheets of foaming cascades; its banks occasionally blackened with masses of scoriated rock, and found a good encampment on the verge of an open bottom, which had been an old camping ground of Cayuse Indians. A great number of deer horns were lying about indicating game in the neighborhood. The timber was uniformly large; some of the pines measuring 22 feet in circumference at the ground and 12 to 13 feet at 6 feet above.

> In all our journeying, we had never traveled through a country where the rivers were so abounding in falls, and the name of the stream is singularly characteristic. At everyplace where we come in the neighborhood of the river is heard the roaring of the falls. The rock along the banks of the stream and the ledge over which it falls, is a scoriated basalt with a bright metallic fracture. The stream goes over in one clear pitch succeeded by a foaming cataract of several hundred yards. In the

little bottom above the falls, a small stream discharges and disappears below.

December 6. The morning was frosty and clear. We continued up the stream on an undulating forest ground, over which there was scattered much fallen timber. We met here a village of Nez Perce Indians who appeared to be coming down from the mountains and had with them fine bands of horses. With them were a few Snake Indians of the root digging species. From the forest we emerged into an open valley 10 or 12 miles wide, through which the stream was flowing tranquilly, upward of 200 feet broad, with occasional islands, and bordered with fine broad bottoms, crossing the river, which here issues from a great mountain ridge on the right, we continued up the southern and smaller branch over a level country, consisting of a fine meadowland, alternating with pine forests and encamped on it early in the evening. A warm sunshine made the day pleasant.

December 7. Today we had good traveling ground; the trail leading sometimes over rather sandy soils in the pine forests and sometimes over meadowland along the stream. The great beauty of the country in summer constantly suggested itself to our imagination; and even now we found it beautiful as we rode along these meadows from a half a mile to two miles wide. The rich soil and the excellent water surrounded by noble forest, make a picture that would delight the eye of a farmer, and I regret that the very small scale map would not allow us to give some representation of these features of the country.

December 8. Today we crossed the last branch of the Fall River, issuing, like all others we had crossed in a southwesterly direction from the mountains. Our direction was a little east of south, the train leading constantly through pine forests. The soil was generally bare, consisting, in greater part of a yellowish white pumice stone producing varieties of magnificent pines but not a blade of grass; and tonight our horses were obliged to do without food and use snow for water. These pines are remarkable for the red color of the balls; and among them occurs a species of which the Indians had informed me when leaving the Dalles. The unusual size of the cone (16 or 18 inches long) had attracted their attention; and they pointed it out to me among the curiosities of the country. (The trees) are more remarkable for their large diameter than their height, which usually only averages about 120 feet. The leaflets are short, only 2 or 3 inches long, and 5 in a sheath; the bark of a red color.

Fremont very clearly outlined his travels as he headed south from the Bend area, moving through the majestic pine forests of central Oregon. He remarks on the pumice soils to be found in our area. He also notes the lack of undergrowth and vegetation caused by the frequent natural wildfires that swept through the area. He was obviously impressed with the size of the native ponderosa pine and sugar pine *(Pinus lambertina)* to be found in this area.

An example of the size of these trees can be seen today in the La Pine State Recreation Area where a huge ponderosa pine tree has been preserved.

Fremont traveled southeast into the Great Basin country of Oregon. He was astute enough to recognize this as a basin and was the first to name it as such. He traveled south into Nevada and California crossing into the San Joaquin River Valley, then passed into southern California and returned to Independence, Missouri via the Colorado River, Utah and what are now the states of Colorado and Kansas.

This expedition was also a success. He was the first person to define and label the Great Basin. The maps from his expedition drawn by Charles Preuss were remarkable and important. Fremont's report created a sensation across the country and was exploited by proponents of Manifest Destiny as a guide to the settling of western America. The journal of his trek across the plains was printed in book form and many copies were used by emigrating pioneers as their "guide book" as they headed west for new lives in the "Oregon country" over the next 25 years.

Fremont went on to later explorations and fame. His experiences led him to be nominated by the Republicans in 1856 for the Presidency. He attained the rank of Major General in the Civil War. He died in 1890.

Next in the series of explorers was the Williamson-Abbot expedition, which was one of the Pacific Railroad Surveys authorized by Congress. Williamson and Abbot traveled through central Oregon in the summer of 1855. There was a national debate taking place about the advisability of connecting the eastern states with the west coast by railroad. Congress then authorized a series of expeditions to explore possible routes for this railroad. Prior to the Civil war, a number of explorations were made by the U.S. Army Topographical Engineers. Lieutenant Robert Stockton Williamson and Lieutenant Henry Larcom Abbot were in charge of an expedition whose purpose was to explore the west coast for ways to link up railroad termini along the coast in a north-south fashion. They began in May at Benicia on the Sacramento River northeast of San Francisco. This group of 60 explorers was accompanied by Dr. John Strong Newberry, scientist.

This expedition traveled north through the central valley of

California and entered Oregon into what is now Klamath County. The expedition traveled north exploring for possible railroad routes. Among the participants in this expedition was Lieutenant Phillip Sheridan and Private George Crook who would later go on to earn fame in the Civil Was and the subsequent Indian wars. They traveled through the Klamath Lake and Klamath Marsh area and entered the drainage of the Deschutes River in August of 1855.

From here they proceeded north along the Deschutes River, exploring into the Cascades as they came. The published expedition map, "From the Northern Boundary of California to the Columbia River" includes, for the first time, what is now the area of the National Monument showing Paulina Creek clearly flowing into the Deschutes River. Although Dr. Newberry explored the lower flanks of the river, particularly along the rapids at Benham Falls, he never actually entered the summit caldera of the volcano.

The expedition moved north through central Oregon following, in general, the northward path of the Deschutes River. Indians had been playing hide-and-seek with the party and during some of the encounters, mainly at night, horses were taken from camp. Indians were often seen crouching in the tall grass observing the expedition and its activities. In time the Indians became a threat. To avoid trouble, the explorers arranged to cross the Cascade Range through a little-known pass. The men were guided by an Indian youth who volunteered his information and services.

They reached Portland safely, then started back for California. They ascended the Willamette Valley, crossed the mountains into the Umpqua and Rogue River Valleys and took no side explorations, due to the Rogue Indian Wars then in progress, and headed directly into the Siskiyou Mountains and into California. The venture was successful and the Williamson-Abbot Expedition was one of the final phases of field operations for the Pacific Railroad Survey. This 1855 expedition demonstrated it was possible to connect a transcontinental railroad with branches running north from San Francisco.

In the period following the surveys and the outbreak of the Civil War, there were arguments among politicians as to where the overland route would run — through the northern or southern states — as there were suitable ways through each. But the war stopped all major expansionist construction. It would not be until 1869 that the final spike was driven, in a Transcontinental Railroad at Promontory Point, Utah. The route was one of those outlined in an original Army Corps of Topographical Engineers survey.

In the Pacific Northwest, a route closely following the northbound trek of Williamson and Abbot was eventually built between

Klamath Falls, Bend and the Columbia River. The return trip of the explorers was followed, with a minor exception, with rails planted in the Willamette, Umpqua and Rogue River Valleys and across the Siskiyou Mountains into California.

The final scientific exploration mentioned here was by Israel C. Russell. He was a geologist employed by the U.S. Geologic Survey who traveled through central Oregon in the summer of 1903. His appears to be the earliest scientific, geologic description of Newberry Volcano:

> In the south central part of Crook County (this is before Deschutes County was formed), there stands a dark forested mountain of notable height and a widely expanded base, and the deeply eroded summit of which Paulina and East Lakes are situated. The mountain is surrounded by many lesser elevations, most of which have still recognizable craters, and is connected on its northeast side by the intervening highlands with the Paulina Mountains, as designated on the General Land Office map of Oregon. Reference has already been made to the fact that a large mountain and the eroded summit of which Paulina and East lakes are situated is locally considered part of the Paulina Mountains, and a desirability stated of giving it a separate and individual name. For this purpose none seems more appropriate than that of one of the earlier explorers of Oregon, who did much to make the geography, geology, and botany of the state widely known. I refer to Dr. John Strong Newberry, one of the geologists of the Pacific Railway Survey, and venture to term the mountain in question Mount Newberry in his honor. The sharp culminating peak of Mount Newberry has an elevation of 7,387 feet above the sea. The approximate height of the adjacent portion of the valley of the Deschutes is 4,200 feet making the visual height of the mountain as seen from the west about 3,000 feet. The mountain is prominent from every point of view from which it can be seen and has a greater height than that of the adjacent portion of the crest line of the Cascade Mountains. The base of the mountain is widely extended, its diameter being in the neighborhood of 20 or 25 miles, but is indefinite on all sides except the west because of the associated but lesser mountains and the numerous volcanic craters of recent date that surround it.

Russell delineated much of the structural geology of the volcano. However, some of his conclusions are now considered incorrect, particularly his impression that a glacier had carved much of the volcano. He did recognize that the caldera at Newberry and the caldera at Crater Lake had much in common as to their origins. □

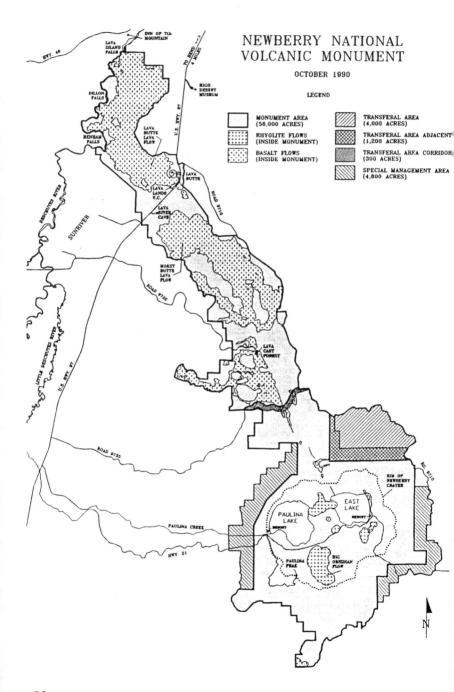

NEWBERRY NATIONAL VOLCANIC MONUMENT

OCTOBER 1990

LEGEND

- MONUMENT AREA (56,000 ACRES)
- RHYOLITE FLOWS (INSIDE MONUMENT)
- BASALT FLOWS (INSIDE MONUMENT)
- TRANSFERAL AREA (4,000 ACRES)
- TRANSFERAL AREA ADJACENT (1,200 ACRES)
- TRANSFERAL AREA CORRIDOR (300 ACRES)
- SPECIAL MANAGEMENT AREA (4,800 ACRES)

Geologic History
of Newberry Volcano

Newberry Volcano has a geologic diversity unsurpassed in the Pacific Northwest and is the largest quaternary (ice-age) volcano by volume in the Northwest. It has the youngest flow of lava in the area and is an example of many aspects of volcanic activity.

As one stands at the summit of Paulina Peak and looks out over the surrounding landscape, everything that one sees is volcanically derived. All the mountain peaks on the western horizon are volcanoes. All the buttes, plains, and hills in any direction are made up of the products of volcanoes. Even the alluvial basins such as Fort Rock and La Pine are filled with products derived from or eroded from volcanoes.

> Newberry is frequently called a "crater," but it is a "caldera" — much different.

Why is this volcano located where it is? What are the forces responsible for constructing it? What are the explanations for the various land forms that can be seen? The answers to these questions have been sought by geologists for many years. Some of them are reasonably well understood. Others are still a mystery. Some of the information that follows is taken from Robert Jensen's *Roadside Guide to the Geology of Newberry Volcano,* 1988, a must for those visitors with an interest in details of Newberry Volcano's geology.

There is much speculation as to why Newberry Volcano is located where it is. The crest of the Cascade Range runs north to south approximately 25 miles to the west of Newberry. The High Cascades (as distinguished from the Western Cascades) are a range of young volcanoes less than 2,000,000 years old. To the south and southeast of Newberry lies the Basin and Range province of North America. This large province extends south through Nevada, Arizona, New Mexico and well into Mexico. This province consists of block-faulted mountains separated by alluvial basins. Walker Rim to the south represents the most northwesterly extent of the Basin and Range province in Oregon. To the east of Newberry lies the High Lava Plains province. This province includes the Brothers Fault Zone which

Geologic Setting of Newberry Volcano

50 MILES

Quaternary and upper Tertiary sedimentary rocks

High Cascade lavas

Olivine basalt plateaus

Stams Mountain volcanic complex

Columbia River Basalt plateaus

Miocene and older volcanics

Fault, hachured side down

Volcano

marks the northern boundary of the Basin and Range province in Oregon. The Brothers Fault Zone has localized volcanic activity over the last 10 million years (m.y.). A well-defined east to west age progression of silicic volcanic domes occurs along the Brothers Fault Zone with ages in excess of 10 m.y. east of Burns to less than 1 m.y. at Newberry.

It is therefore no accident that the Newberry Volcano lies at the intersection of these three geologic provinces. The intersection of fault zones related to these provinces has resulted in localizing volcanism, probably producing the large size of Newberry Volcano.

Newberry caldera (the 5-miles-in-diameter summit feature) is the centerpiece of the volcano. It is important to point out that the formation of a caldera is very different from the formation of a crater. Newberry's caldera is frequently mistakenly referred to as a "crater." In geologic terms, a caldera represents a more-or-less round depression that is formed by collapse. The collapse is caused by withdrawal or eruption from an underlying magma chamber. Large-volume flank eruptions, such as occur in Hawaii, can drain a magma chamber resulting in caldera collapse. Violent summit-area eruptions such as occurred at Crater Lake can eject large volumes of material from the magma chamber and also result in the formation of a caldera. When geologists use the term crater, they are referring to a funnel-shaped depression in the summit of a volcanic cone. This crater is formed by the eruption of material which builds up around the vent forming the depression and there is little or no subsidence associated with magma draining from the magma chamber.

Evidence exists that the geologic history of Newberry is complex and contains multiple episodes of summit collapse. There is evidence that volcanic activity has occurred at the site of Newberry for at least a million years. None of the rocks on Newberry have so far been dated at more than 730,000 years, but intracanyon flows at Cove Palisades, some 50 miles north of Newberry near Madras, are chemically similar and disappear beneath Newberry flows when traced to the south. On the northeast flank of the volcano on the edge of the sagebrush country, one finds unusual rock formations in Tepee Draw. The so-called Tepee Draw Tuff has been radiometrically dated at somewhat over 500,000 years. This welded tuff is a deposit from the earliest recognized caldera-forming event at Newberry. Such tuffs are the result of extremely violent and cataclysmic volcanic eruptions. It is likely that the eruption of this particular rock unit would have destroyed all life for tens to hundreds of square miles around the volcano. The material ejected from the volcano was so hot that it welded together when it was

Lava Butte. Highway 99 crosses picture.

deposited.

At least 3 more deposits from probable caldera-forming events are known on Newberry. Geologists currently believe that Newberry has never been much higher than it is today and that a caldera has been present for much of its geologic history. Today's caldera is believed to be the result of multiple, overlapping collapses that have gradually enlarged the caldera to its present size. The current high point of the volcano, Paulina Peak, represents an extrusion of rhyolite, a high-silica, volcanic rock from a subterranean fracture system. Caldera collapse later occurred along this fracture system. Within the caldera itself there are a variety of volcanic features that will be discussed later.

The flanks of Newberry Volcano are dotted by hundreds of

cinder cones and spatter cones and a few domes. These features vary widely in age. The Monument includes many of Newberry Volcano's youngest cinder and spatter cones and their associated flows. Many of these young vents are located along the Northwest Rift Zone of Newberry which extends from the caldera to the Deschutes River. This zone is a series of fault segments that has long been a zone of weakness along which volcanic activity has occurred. About 6,100 C-14 years ago (approximately 7,000 calendar years), 3 to 5 short eruptive periods associated with vents along this zone produced 11 basaltic (low-silica volcanic rock) lava flows.

One of these young cinder cones and flows is Lava Butte which is near Lava Lands Interpretive Center, the top of which is easily reached by car. But during peak summer tourist season, private cars may not be allowed due to congestion and limited parking at the top. In this event, a shuttle bus takes visitors to the summit where there is a manned Forest Service fire lookout.

As basaltic magma rises, gasses begin to come out of the magma solution and rise toward the top of the magma body so that the first magma to reach the surface is gas-rich. These early gas-rich lavas typically erupt as a curtain of fire a mile or so in length. But in a few hours they begin to localize and to build a cinder cone. At Lava Butte these early events are preserved in the spatter cones and flows east of Highway 97, but have been buried at Lava Butte to the west of the highway,. Due to the prevailing southwest winds, a larger portion of Lava Butte cinders were deposited northeast of the cone. This resulted in the south side being thinner and weaker. As the early gas-rich lavas were depleted, less-fluid lava began to rise into the cinder cone. This pooled-lava then broke through the weak south side. The basalt spread as a series of flows approximately 6 miles to the north and pushed the Deschutes River to the west. The flows covered over 9 square miles and were probably erupted over a period of a few months or even a few years.

As travelers on Highway 97 drive past Lava Butte, they notice not only the craggy, rough lava (called ''aa'' — a Hawaiian term for rough lava) flow southeast of the butte, but also the wind-blown cinders north of Lava Butte. It has been estimated that of the total amount of material erupted from Lava Butte, 90 percent of it is found in the lava flows, 9 percent in the cinders of the butte itself and 1 percent in the air-fall material to the northeast.

If one stands on the top of Lava Butte and looks to the southeast towards Newberry, it is quite easy to notice the shield-shaped configuration of the volcano. The shield-shape is classically seen in the basaltic volcanoes of the Hawaiian Islands; however, Newberry

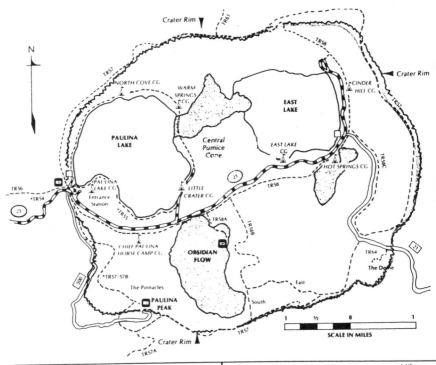

NATIONAL FOREST CAMPGROUNDS	Units
PAULINA LAKE	64
NORTH COVE*	6
WARM SPRINGS*	5
LITTLE CRATER	53
EAST LAKE	29
HOT SPRINGS	43
CINDER HILL	105
CHIEF PAULINA HORSE CAMP	13

*No Drinking Water;
Accessible by Boat or Trail Only.

LEGEND

Entrance Station		View Point	
Campground		Paved Road	
Cindered Road		Resort	
Lava Flow		Private Land	
		Trail	- - - - -

	TRAILS	Miles
No.	Description	(One-Way)
*TR54	Paulina Falls Trail	0.3
*TR55	Paulina Lake Shore Loop	7.5
TR56	Peter Skene Ogden Trail	8.6
TR57	Newberry Crater Rim Trail (round trip)	21.0
TR57A	From TR57 south to Road 2225	1.2
TR57B	From Entrance Station southeast to Paulina Pk	3.5
TR58	From Paulina Crk. Bridge east through Newberry Crater to TR57	8.5
TR58A	Obsidian Flow Trail	0.3
TR58B	Lost Lake Trail south	2.5
TR58B	Lost Lake Trail east	3.5
TR58C	Parallels Road 21 from East Lake Resort to TR57	2.0
TR61	From TR57 to Swamp Wells	8.0
*TR64	Dome Trail	0.5

*Hiker Trail Only

Map of Newberry Caldera

Paulina Falls. North and south falls are separated by small island. Rocks, at bottom of north fall were eroded by force of the water, were once at top of the falls. The drop is 80-feet. Photographed from visitor viewing area.

is not a true shield-volcano. It is instead made up of low and high-silica rock types. The low-silica (basaltic) rocks form fluid lava flows that spread without steep gradients. The high-silica (rhyolitic) rocks, when erupted in large volumes, also typically form ashflows which do not have steep gradients. Andesite and basaltic-andesite flows are of a more intermediate composition and tend to form the steeper sided cones such as the Three Sisters and Mount Hood, common in the High Cascades.

Because the High Cascade volcanoes are higher than Newberry and do not lie in the rain shadow of another mountain range, they have been sculpted and deeply eroded by the action of glaciers over the last million years. There is no evidence that Newberry has ever been glaciated despite such speculation by early geologists.

Just prior to entering the caldera from the west, a parking lot for Paulina Falls is noted. A short hike leads to a spectacular overlook of these 80-foot falls. The cliffs over which the falls drop are another deposit erupted during one of Newberry's cataclysmic caldera-forming eruptions. Geologic processes are ongoing even if infre-

Paulina Lake and Paulina Peak, the mountain reflected in a puddle from melted snow in May.

quent. In 1983 a large section of the cliff between the two falls fell, exposing fresh, reddish rock. The older, exposed rock is covered with a white carbonate coating that is deposited over time.

At the west edge of the caldera, a road to the south goes to the top of Paulina Peak. This road is an extremely scenic drive to the 7,985 ft. summit. During the typical summer season this access road is usually passable in a high-clearance vehicle; however, travelers who shun heights and exposures are cautioned that this may not be the road for them. There are hairpin twists and turns on the very low-speed, rough, gravel-road. If one meets another vehicle, it may be necessary to back some distance before one finds a place to pass.

The only speed on this road must be s-l-o-w!

Paulina Peak is the third highest spot that one can drive to in the state of Oregon. It is arguably the best view in the entire state. Looking to the west one sees the entire Cascade Range from Mount Adams in Washington state to Mount Shasta in California.

To the east and southeast lies Oregon's high desert, a land of sagebrush and juniper-covered volcanic rocks. On an extremely clear day, utilizing binoculars or a spotting scope, the escarpments of Hart Mountain and Steens Mountain can be observed. To the southeast is the basin of ancient Fort Rock Lake, which held a 300 foot deep lake about 20,000 years ago. The lake has probably been dry the majority of the last 10,000 years. The basin currently has no outlet to the ocean and is indeed a part of the Great Basin. The presence of fossil salmonid bones indicate that at one time in the past there was a connection with a stream that gave access to the Pacific Ocean. This would have allowed passage of anadromous fish — those fish that migrate from an ocean up stream to spawn. This early outlet has yet to be located.

To the northeast lie the Ochoco and Blue Mountains and to the north the basin of the Deschutes River. To the immediate west is the La Pine basin which contains volcanic sedimentary deposits at least 1,300 feet deep. Some of the surface deposits are lake beds formed when flows from Lava Butte dammed the Deschutes River near Benham Falls. This dam backed up the river and formed a shallow lake that covered much of the Sunriver area.

Within the caldera, one's attention is drawn to the two lakes, East and Paulina. Paulina Lake covers an area of approximately 1,530 acres and has a maximum depth of 250 feet, while East Lake covers an area of approximately 1,050 acres and has a maximum depth of 180 feet. The lakes are the surface expression of ground water trapped within the bounding faults of the caldera. There are no surface inlets to either lake. All lake water comes from precipitation (rain and snow) within the caldera. There are no drainages from East Lake into Paulina Lake. Nearly one mile separates the lakes. Paulina Lake discharges into Paulina Creek. Both lakes have drowned hot springs in them and on the southeastern shore of East Lake is a particularly active area of vents where the smell of sulfur can be detected. During the early 20th century, the East Lake Health Resort was located in this area but little of this remains after a disastrous fire in 1923. (The present-day East Lake Fishing Resort is unrelated.) Similar hot springs occur in the northeastern part of Paulina Lake.

The caldera of Newberry Volcano is a geologic wonderland of lava flows, ash flows, pumice cones, and tuff cones. The most pro-

Paulina Lake (foreground) and East Lake from Paulina Peak.

minent flow in the caldera is the Big Obsidian Flow, which also happens to be the youngest dated flow in the state of Oregon. It erupted approximately 1,300 years ago and not only produced the magnificent obsidian and rhyolite flow visible, but also spread an ash flow into Paulina Lake and spread out a large amount of pumice that covers the southern part of the caldera. A plume of this deposit extends over 40 miles to the east.

Another prominent feature of the caldera is the Central Pumice Cone. This 6,700-year-old cone once contained a lava lake which drained to form the Game Hut Obsidian Flow on the south side of the cone. The Interlake Obsidian Flow is also about 6,700 years old and is located north of the Central Pumice Cone. Southeast of East Lake are two 3,500-year-old obsidian flows.

Although these flows are called "obsidian," they are a complex mix of obsidian, pumice and rhyolite. Chemically, they are rhyolitic in composition. However, the name applied to a particular piece of rock depends on its cooling history and the gas content at the time of eruption. As with basaltic eruptions, the early part of a rhyolitic eruption is typically highly gas-charged, but because rhyolite is so sticky the resulting eruption is extremely violent and can produce large deposits of air-fall and ashflow pumice. Later in the eruption, as degassed magma reaches the surface, massive flows of rhyolite occur. Under conditions that are not well-understood, portions of these flows may form obsidian. The darker color of obsidian is due to its iron content.

South of the Central Pumice Cone and east of the Big Obsidian Flow is the location of the U.S. Geological Survey Newberry Well No. 2. This well was drilled in 1981 to a depth of 3,058 feet and yielded temperatures of 509 degrees Fahrenheit. Geologists learned from this well that Newberry caldera was once deeper than it is today. The first 1,640 feet of drilling consisted of caldera-fill deposits made up of sediments and caldera eruptive products. As Jensen notes, the flows below 1,640 feet are similar to the flows on the flanks of the volcano and may be the former upper part of the volcano that collapsed to form the caldera.

One of the more interesting and unusual types of volcanoes that occur in association with Newberry Volcano is the tuff-ring or maar. "Maar" is the German term for this type of volcano. The chemical composition of the palagonite tuff making up these volcanoes is the same as that of basaltic cinder cones. The difference arises from the fact that these types of volcanoes are formed when rising basaltic magma comes into contact with abundant ground water. The resulting contact generates violent steam explosions which drive muddy slurries of fractured rock away from the vent, producing low, ring-like structures. These maar volcanoes only occur in areas where ground water is abundant. Little Crater, along the shore of Paulina Lake, is an excellent example. Another is along the southeast flank of Newberry in the Fort Rock Basin where Fort Rock and Hole-in-the-Ground are good examples. □

The Plant Life of Newberry Volcano

The Pacific Northwest has a reputation as an area of high precipitation. This is particularly true in areas west of the Cascade Mountains. However, the Cascades are a moisture barrier that wrings the water from the air as it passes over the mountains. This drier air drops down into the higher, cooler plateaus on the east side. Newberry Volcano is located in this transition zone. It lies in a transition from the conifer forests of the eastern slopes of the Cascades to the juniper woodlands and shrub steppe of Oregon's "High Desert."

This mixing and matching of vegetation communities provides a wonderful opportunity for plant lovers. Sugar pine *(Pinus lambertina),* a conifer more common to the south and California, is found growing in significant stands in the Newberry area but it is infrequently found north of Newberry. Just south of Newberry are the northernmost stands of Shasta red fir. *(Abies magnifica variety shastina).*

Summer storms tend to drop more rain in these higher elevations and winter storms also tend to accumulate more snow on the higher peaks. This means that conifers are found further to the east on Newberry Volcano than they are either north or south of this mountain. The forest transition zone to the east of the volcano is abrupt and dramatic. This rather sharp tree-line reminds us of the importance of moisture for the growth of forests. To the east side of Newberry, many sites are marginal forest lands due to low precipitation.

Precipitation may range from a yearly average of 30 to 40 inches per year at the caldera to 6 to 8 inches out on the eastern fringes. Due to this diversity of weather, rainfall, slope aspect and geology, there is an accompanying difference in plant life.

The lowest elevations of this national monument occur along the Deschutes River. These are pristine riparian areas with willow, aspen, and sedges in abundance. The river here is unchanged by the impacts of man. Access is difficult as there is no road. Only a few boaters, canoeists, kayakers, and anglers traverse this stretch. Beaver can be seen and osprey swoop to fish along the stream; elk and deer occasionally wander along the banks. Magnificent ponderosa pine *(Pinus ponderosa)* grow along the stream.* These mighty trees occupy the lower elevations of the pine forests of the monument.

Ponderosa Pine

At the time white settlers arrived in central Oregon, the lower elevations of what is now the Monument, 3,500-ft. - 5,000-ft. elevations, were nothing but unending forests of thick-barked "yellow belly" ponderosa pines. These trees were widely and evenly spac-

*David Douglas (1798-1834) Scottish botanist who traveled in North America, is generally associated with the Douglas fir tree which was named for him. It is Douglas who first noted and named the ponderosa pine after visiting a stand of this tall pine tree along the Spokane River in 1830.

Ponderosa pine

ed with trunks measuring from 3 to 4-feet in diameter. Many trees had no branches for the first 50-feet above the ground. These trees would average from 100-feet to 130-feet in height. There was very little undergrowth found on the forest floor.

These plant communities were maintained by fire and wildfires were a natural and regular visitor to this tree community. The ponderosa pine, in its mature stages, has thick bark that can stand a hot fire with little damage. The lack of lower branches prevented fire from getting into the crown of the tree causing a so-called "crown fire." A crown fire can destroy an entire forest.

Dr. Joyce Bork, Ph.D., formerly of Central Oregon Community College in Bend, studied fire frequency in the central Oregon ponderosa pine forests. Her findings indicate that fire was a regular visitor — every 8 to 12 years — in these stands. These fires would be of low intensity and would burn the accumulated pine needles (duff), fallen branches, and herbaceous vegetation of the forest floor.

Mature ponderosa pine with defoliated crown which may have been result of fungal rust. (Right) Closeup of identifying bark. (Center) Bark flakes off tree and falls (lower) onto forest floor. Tree is near entrance of Lava Cast Forest.

Old style logging.

It would then be a number of years before the next fire would visit this site allowing for another build-up of the "duff." Pre-historically, it was unusual to see a stand-replacement type of fire which would destroy the entire plant community. If a windstorm, an insect infestation, or unusual fire should destroy these trees, a young ponderosa pine forest would re-establish in a few years. It would then grow, over time, to a new magnificent ponderosa pine forest. By process of elimination, the frequent fires sweeping through these young trees would thin out the stand and gradually turn the stand into one having the characteristics of an ancient forest.

It was this magnificent timber resource that drew large economic interests to the city of Bend (founded in the 1880's). The local pine forests were the last on the continent, and, beginning in 1916 were utilized heavily to the advantage of the economy of Bend. Billions of board feet of high-quality boards of old-growth pine were turned out from the mills in and about Bend. Only recently have we almost reached the end of this magnificent resource. Under

Twisted ponderosa pine tree in crater atop Lava Butte.

Remnant of a happier life. Ponderosa pine "snag" near base of Lava Butte.

pressure from a wide array of groups, the National Forests are making efforts to maintain the last stands of these ancient forests. The lower elevations of the Monument will be managed to recreate these magnificent climax ponderosa pine forests.

Early settlers describe various aspects of the fire climax ponderosa pine forest. Most of them mention a noticeable lack of diversity of animal and plant life; deer were not abundant in the original forests. Few birds or other animals were observed. This did not mean such forests were a sterile or monotonous community. These pine forests were undoubtedly structured into a mosaic of classes due to such things as fire, insects, and other factors. There are a number of species highly associated with climax forests. These include the white-headed woodpecker and the flammulated owls.

One insect dependent on the ponderosa pine is the Pandora Moth *(Coloradia Pandora)*. This beautiful, large, 4-inch wingspan moth is found at low population levels in the pine forest each year. About every 20 years, it reaches epidemic proportions. The Pandora moth has an unusual 2-year life cycle whereby moth-flight, mating and egg-laying occurs in one year and defoliation by caterpillars happens in the next. In the year of defoliation, the caterpillars do most of their feeding on old needles in the spring. In June, the large caterpillars climb down the trunks of trees then burrow into the ground where a pupa forms. The insect rests in the pupal stage for the next 12 months with adult moths emerging the next summer to begin the cycle again. During those periods, when the Pandora moth is in epidemic status, caterpillars often defoliate trees so severely that many appear to be dead. Shortly after defoliation, however, spring growth refoliates the trees and only a few weakened individuals die. Indians acquainted with these outbreaks (even in modern times) collected and roasted the caterpillars for eating and considered them a delicacy.

Two bark beetles are also significant inspect pests in ponderosa pine forests. The western pine beetle *(Dendroctonus brevicomis)* prefers mature trees but will attack pole-size ones. The mountain pine beetle *(Dendroctonus ponderosae)* favors second growth pine but sometimes will attack large mature trees. Both beetles mine their way under the bark and kill the trees by obstructing water and nutrient-conducting tissues. Most of the time trees are killed individually. In outbreak-episodes, trees are killed in large numbers.

Many people in central Oregon feel that there is nothing more attractive than a mature stand of orange-yellow barked ponderosa pines. These mature trees are referred to as "yellow-bellies" or

Forest fires get started by lightning strikes as well as by today's careless campers. Historically, fires cleaned the forest floor of debris, killed troublesome insects and in some cases, fires aid tree health.

"pumpkins." The bark scales off in puzzle-shaped pieces. The yellowish-orange cast to the bark is imparted by a pigment. This pigment is obscured in the younger trees. In fact, young ponderosa pines are frequently referred to as black-bark pine. This is because there is a very dark water-soluble pigment in the bark of the ponderosa pine. When the tree is young and fast growing, the bark is shed rapidly and there is not an opportunity for this dark water-soluble pigment to be washed from the bark. However, as the tree gets older and growth slows, the bark stays on the tree longer. This allows the water-soluble dark pigment to be washed from the bark and the orange color of the bark becomes dominant. As bark flakes from the tree it accumulates around the base of the tree. Periodic fires eliminate this mount of flammable material at the tree base. If fire is not a regular visitor, too much can gather and during an infrequent fire which burns hot, the base of the tree can actually be scorched and could kill the tree. The ponderosa pine was named by Scottish botanist David Douglas because of its great "ponderous" size. The needles grow in clusters of three and are much longer than the neighboring lodgepole pines.

To the east of Newberry volcano, ponderosa pines disappear in areas where the rainfall is less than 12 inches a year. The cones from this grand tree range from 2 to 6 inches long and are prickly to the fingers. The seeds from pine cones are a favorite food of ground squirrels. As we have seen, the stand of pine timber resist fire but the pine cones, when ignited, become nearly white-hot.

Lodgepole Pine

Lodgepole pine *(Pinus contorta)* grows above the elevation of ponderosa pine and apparently got its name because Indians used the tall, narrow, straight trunks of this tree as poles for their giant tepee-lodges.

Although ponderosa pine is somewhat frost tolerant, lodgepole pine is more so and can grow in higher, colder elevations. This tree does not approach the grand stature of the magnificent ponderosa and it has a shorter life. Whereas "old" ponderosa may live to be three to four hundred years, an "old" lodgepole may attain somewhere between one hundred to one hundred fifty years of age.

Fire was also a frequent visitor to lodgepole pine forests. Although very sensitive to any fire, due to its thin bark, this species is very opportunistic and readily re-invades areas denuded by fire or insects.

Lodgepole pine is very susceptible to the mountain pine beetle and it is appropriate to go into greater detail on the life cycle of this forest insect which is found throughout the West.

The mountain pine beetle *(Dendroctonus ponderosae)* is found at all times in the lodgepole forest. But when a lodgepole pine forest is stressed by competition for sunlight and nutrients, or it reaches old age, this insect pest can be found in epidemic levels in the forest.

In the 1980's, central Oregon experienced such an outbreak and millions of lodgepole pines were killed throughout the forests. These dead, standing trees have created an ideal situation for fire. In prehistoric times, a lightning strike would have started a fire which may have burned tens of thousands of acres at one time. With current fire management strategies, these large fires no longer occur.

The mountain pine beetle is a small insect, about the size of a grain of rice, but is remarkably adapted to attacking lodgepole pine trees. It is genetically programmed to fly to weakened trees of a certain age and class. Once the flying insects find a tree that is susceptible, they lure other insects to that tree, and to adjacent trees, by secreting pheromones, an airborne attractant molecule. Shortly, these insects lay eggs underneath the bark. A white, legless, grublike larva hatches from the eggs and mines in the soft cambium tissue between the bark and the wood.

The beetle also carries one or more species of blue-stain fungus (mostly species of *Ceratocystis*) which invade the sapwood. What kills the tree is the combined effect of the larval-mining and the water-conducting tissue being plugged with the blue-stain fungus. The first evidences of the attack are pitch tubes on the trunk. These are small globules of pitch which are formed as the tree tries to repair the wounds from the attacking beetles. Signs of infestation occur when the needles turn red and eventually drop off the tree. In order of decreasing preference, the beetles prefer lodgepole pine, ponderosa pine, and sugar pines. They also attack and kill western white pine and white bark pine at high elevations. In a typical outbreak, a large number of mature trees, usually 80 years old or older, are generally killed. There's little that can be done to protect single trees of the forests from this forest pest. Good silviculture practices and healthy forests are the best protection from nearly all bark beetles, including the mountain pine beetle.

After infestation with the mountain pine beetle, frequently 90 to 100 percent of the trees larger than 9-inches in diameter will have been killed. These dead, standing trees gradually begin to fall after about 6 years and the fallen trees, branches and pine needles are excellent tinder. A careless person or a lightning strike has a high pro-

Paulina Peak framed by lodgepole pines, clouds, snow in spring.

bability of setting off a major conflagration. As has been previously noted, large fires in the lodgepole pine forests were frequent prior to white man's arrival. Fire is one way this type of forest has of renewing itself. The cones of lodgepole pine are frequently serotinous. This means that after a fire, the cones will open and spread their seeds into the ash bed. Under the right conditions, a new crop of vigorous lodgepole pine seedlings will be growing thickly. The cycle begins anew.

As one ascends in elevation through the Monument one enters the mixed conifer zone. To a great degree the trees in this zone consist of mountain hemlock *(Tsuga mertensiana)* and white fir *(Abies concolor)*. Mountain hemlock is a beautiful tree with small, lacy needles. Hemlocks can be spotted because their terminal leaders tend to droop. *Abies concolor* is a true fir with flat sprays of needles usually with a waxy band of white pores on top called stomata.

White bark pine *(Pinus albicaulis)* is found in the highest elevations of the Monument. It differs from ponderosa pine and lodgepole pine in that each bundle of needles has five instead of two or three needles respectively.

At the summit of Paulina Peak, trees of this species are noted with branches only on one side. This phenomenon is caused by ice

49

crystals in winter winds. In this fashion, the windward sides of these trees are annually denuded. This action favors needles that grow on the lee side of the tree. These are so-called "flag" trees. In extreme conditions, the *krummholz* forms are seen. These trees are gnarled and low-growing. This term is taken from the German language, meaning "twisted wood." *(Krumm* = twisted; *holz* = wood.) Some of these trees can be quite old although not as ancient as their distant cousins, the bristlecone pines *(Pinus aristata)* of the Great Basin.

The cones from white bark pine actually disintegrate on the trees. These cones are a favorite food of the Clark's Nutcracker. Research by Dr. Ron Lanner of the University of Nevada (Reno), has shown that this bird plays an important role in planting the seeds of this tree. Nutcrackers plant caches of these seeds in windswept areas high in the mountains. This frequently gives rise to a multi-trunked grove of white bark pines that are a combination of four or five trees that all sprouted from the seeds in the cache.

Wildflowers

Throughout the Monument are lots of wildflowers. In June and in July the riparian areas along the Deschutes River exhibit tremendous wildflower diversity. In the higher elevations, during July and August, particularly in the caldera and on Paulina Peak, there is a great presentation of colorful wildflowers.

The road to Paulina Peak has excellent displays of rock penstemon *(Penstemon davidsonii)* and Nuttall's linanthastrum *(Linasthastrum nuttallii)*.

Dryer, lower elevations of the Monument host small blue lupines *(Lupinus lepidus var. lobbii)* and purple monkey flower *(Mimulus nanus)*.

One of the more unusual but important plants seen in the Monument is the Oregon pumice grape fern *(Botrychium pumicola)*. This plant is not found elsewhere in the world with the exception of Oregon. In Oregon it grows in only three locations — all in central Oregon:

> Newberry Volcano
> Crater Lake National Park
> Broken Top Volcano in Three Sisters Wilderness

This unusual plant is a relative of the ferns. Most members of the fern family grow in moist areas, however, this plant has adapted to the harsh, windswept environment of high-altitude, pumice scree slopes, and in lodgepole pine forests. Recent surveys by Deschutes National Forest Service personnel found this plant growing lower in the lodgepole pine forests. The Oregon pumice grape fern is one of the rarest plants in Oregon and is awaiting listing on both state and federal endangered species lists.

Wildlife in the National Monument

A number of large mammals live in and travel through the National Monument. Bears are occasionally seen within the caldera. They tend to be secretive and usually only a glimpse is caught of them. It is, however, a good idea to observe care in storing your food.

Elk are also present in the National Monument. They occur both in the caldera area and on the flanks of the volcano. Watch for their large hoofed tracks as you walk in either dusty or muddy areas. They prefer higher elevations during the summer and lower elevations during the winter. Mule deer are found throughout the Monument at almost any time of the year. Part of the winter deer range lies within the Monument boundaries and in wintertime on the eastern part of the forest large numbers of deer can be seen.

The bird life in the Monument is no less than remarkable. Within the caldera, bald eagles can frequently be seen. There has been at least one active bald eagle nest in the caldera in recent times. There is nothing more exciting than seeing America's symbol fly over your head while you're walking along the beach or fishing on the lake.

Ospreys can also be seen fishing at lakes. These beautiful birds are world travelers. In the fall they gather and fly to South America for the winter. They spend the winter feeding in that area and gradually make their way to North America once more. There are osprey nests on the upper reaches of the volcano.

Although peregrine falcons have been seen in the area for some time, the caldera is considered prime nesting habitat and it is possible that falcons will take up residence. □

Immature osprey.

Birds of the
Deschutes National Forest

Birders love to visit Deschutes National Forest and Newberry Volcano to see which birds they can identify. Many birders are looking for the rare birds and feel their day has been made when they spy one. The rarest in the forest are Arctic Loon, White-winged Scoter, Peregrine Falcon, Band-winged Pigeon, Burrowing Owl, Chestnut-backed Chickadee, Mockingbird, and White-winged Crossbill. Of these, most are migrants merely passing through in spring and fall. One should be cautious about thinking that all migrants are rare because there are many seasonal passers-through that are commonly seen:

Common Loon	Ruddy Duck	Myrtle Warbler
Lesser Western Goose	Sandhill Crane	Orange-crowned Warbler
Cackling Canada Goose	Semipalmated Plover	Townsend's Warbler
White-fronted Goose	Least Sandpiper	Hermit Warbler
Snow Goose	Western Sandpiper	Golden-crowned Sparrow
Green-winged Teal	Bonaparte's Gull	Varied Thrush

Birds least seen are the winter visitors. This is not because there are fewer birds but because fewer human visitors are in the forest to see them in winter. This is especially true in the upper elevations (Newberry caldera) because the road is generally snowed-in and human access is possible only by skis or snowmobiles.

Barn Swallows.

The birds listed as winter visitors:

Whistling Swan	Lesser Scaup	Northern Shrike
American Widgeon	Common Goldeneye	Pine Grosbeak
Redhead	Rough-legged Hawk	Slate-colored Junco
Canvasback	Water Pipit	Harris Sparrow
Greater Scaup	Bohemian Waxwing	

The easiest to spot are the yearlong resident birds. Of the 200 birds on our list, 80 of them are year-rounders. In our master list, these are marked "R." The inventory of all known birds in the forest is presented alphabetically.

Birds observed in or within 5 miles of the forest boundary (not necessarily within the National Monument):

M - Migrant Spring and Fall   WV - Winter Visitor
SV - Summer Visitor   R - Resident (all year)

—A—

M	Arctic Loon (rare)
SV	American Bittern
R	American Coot
WV	American Widgeon
SV	Ash-throated Flycatcher
SV	Audubon's Warbler

—B—

R	Bald Eagle
SV	Band-tailed Pigeon (rare)
SV	Barn Swallow
R	Barrow's Goldeneye
R	Belted Kingfisher
SV	Black Tern

R	Black-backed Three-Toed Woodpecker
R	Black-billed Magpie
R	Black-capped Chickadee
SV	Black-crowned Night Heron
SV	Black-headed Grosbeak
SV	Black-throated Gray Warbler
R	Blue Grouse
SV	Blue-winged Teal
WV	Bohemian Waxwing
M	Bonaparte's Gull
R	Brewer's Blackbird

53

Suzi Lewis, a Forest Service Interpretative Naturalist, holds a juvenile great horned owl. This bird sustained a broken wing when its nest, and the tree it was in, was blown down during a storm.

S V	Brewer's Sparrow
R	Brown Creeper
S V	Brown-headed Cowbird
R	Bufflehead
S V	Bullock's Oriole
S V	Burrowing Owl

—C—

M	Cackling Canada Goose
S V	California Gull
R	California Quail
S V	Calliope Hummingbird
R	Canada Goose
R	Canyon Wren
W V	Canvasback
R	Cassin's Finch
R	Cedar Waxwing
S V	Chestnut-backed Chickadee (rare)

S V	Chipping Sparrow
S V	Cinnamon Teal
R	Clark's Nutcracker
S V	Cliff Swallow
R	Common Bushtit
R	Common Crow
S V	Common Egret
W V	Common Goldeneye
M	Common Loon
R	Common Merganser
S V	Common Nighthawk
R	Common Raven
R	Common Snipe
R	Cooper's Hawk

—D—

R	Dipper
S V	Double-crested Cormorant

Female Mountain Bluebird.

R	Downy Woodpecker
S V	Dusky Flycatcher

—E—

S V	Eared Grebe
S V	Eastern Kingbird
R	Evening Grosbeak

—F—

R	Ferruginous Hawk
S V	Forster's Tern
S V	Fox Sparrow

—G—

S V	Gadwall
R	Golden Eagle
S V	Golden-crowned Kinglet
M S	Golden-crowned Sparrow
R	Goshawk
S V	Gray Flycatcher
R	Gray Jay
S V	Gray-crowned Rosy Finch
R	Great Blue Heron
R	Great Grey Owl (rare)
R	Great Horned Owl
S V	Greater Scaup
S V	Green-tailed Towhee
M	Green-winged Teal

—H—

R	Hairy Woodpecker
S V	Hammond's Flycatcher
W V	Harris Sparrow (rare)
S V	Hermit Thrush

M	Hermit Warbler
R	Hooded Merganser
R	Horned Lark
R	House Finch
R	House Sparrow
S V	House Wren

—L—

M	Least Sandpiper
M	Lesser Canada Goose
W V	Lesser Scaup
S V	Lewis' Woodpecker
S V	Lincoln's Sparrow
S V	Loggerhead Shrike
S V	Long-billed Marsh Wren
R	Long-eared Owl

—M—

SV	MacGillivray's Warbler
R	Mallard
SV	Marsh Hawk
M	Mockingbird (rare)
R	Mountain Bluebird
R	Mountain Chickadee
R	Mountain Quail
R, SV	Mourning Dove
M	Myrtle Warbler

—N—

W V	Northern Shrike
R	Northern Three-toed Woodpecker

55

Common Loon.

—O—

SV	Olive-sided Flycatcher
M	Orange-crowned Warbler
R	Oregon Junco
SV	Osprey

—P—

SV	Peregrine Falcon (rare)
SV	Pied-billed Grebe
R	Pileated Woodpecker
WV	Pine Grosbeak
R	Pine Siskin
R	Piñon Jay
SV	Pintail
SV	Poor-will
R	Prairie Falcon
R	Purple Finch
R	Pygmy Nuthatch
R	Pygmy Owl

—R—

R	Red-breasted Nuthatch
R	Red Crossbill
R	Red-shafted Flicker
R	Red-tailed Hawk
R	Red-winged Blackbird
SV	Ring-billed Gull
R	Ring-necked Duck
R	Robin
R	Rock Dove
SV	Rock Wren
WV	Rough-legged Hawk
SV	Ruby-crowned Kinglet
M	Ruddy Duck
R	Ruffed Grouse

Great Blue Heron.

SV	Rufous Hummingbird
WV	Rufous-sided Towhee

—S—

R	Sage Grouse
SV	Sage Sparrow
SV	Sage Thrasher
M	Sandhill Crane
SV	Savannah Sparrow
R	Saw-whet Owl
SV	Say's Phoebe
R	Screech Owl
M	Semipalmated Plover
R	Sharp-shinned Hawk
SV	Shoveler
WV	Slate-colored Junco
M	Snow Goose
SV	Solitary Vireo
R	Song Sparrow
SV	Sora Rail
R	Sparrow Hawk
SV	Spotted Sandpiper

R	Starling
R	Steller's Jay
R	Swainson's Hawk

—T—

R	Townsend's Solitaire
M	Townsend's Warbler
SV	Traill's Flycatcher
SV	Tree Swallow
R	Turkey (introduced Green Ridge area)
SV	Turkey Vulture

—V—

M, SV	Varied Thrush
SV	Vaux's Swift
SV	Violet-green Swallow
SV	Virginia Rail

—W—

SV	Warbling Vireo
WV	Water Pipit
R	Western Bluebird
R	Western Canada Goose
SV	Western Grebe
SV	Western Kingbird
R	Western Meadowlark
M	Western Sandpiper
V	Western Tanager
SV	Western Wood Pewee
WV	Whistling Swan
SV	White Pelican
R	White-breasted Nuthatch
SV	White-crowned Sparrow
M	White-fronted Goose
R	White-headed Woodpecker
SV	White-throated Swift (Fort Rock)
M	White-winged Crossbill (rare)
M	White-winged Scoter (rare)
SV	Williamson's Sapsucker
SV	Wilson's Phalarope
SV	Wilson's Warbler
R	Winter Wren
SV	Wood Duck

—Y—

SV	Yellow-bellied Sapsucker
SV	Yellow-bellied Sapsucker (red-breasted race)
SV	Yellow-headed Blackbird
SV	Yellowthroat
SV	Yellow Warbler

Early Development
in the Newberry Area

The area around Bend and south along the Deschutes River was not settled until the 1870's. John Y. Todd, an early cattleman, built the first bridge across the Deschutes River at Sherar's Falls about 1860. He arrived in the Bend region in 1877 and purchased the Farewell Bend Ranch at the south end of town. Todd had a cabin on the Upper Deschutes basin in 1879 but he moved on to Prineville and then to the Willamette Valley about the turn of the century.

Todd is well-remembered because his ranch, Farewell Bend, was the name adopted for the town. But the Post Office Department, Washington, D.C. declined the name as it could be confused with another post office of the same name in Malheur County. The local postmaster, William H. Staats, wanted to rename the office Pilot Butte, but that was also rejected and replaced with Deschutes. By 1904 all this shuffle was finished and the Bend, Oregon post office was finally and firmly established.

Another early rancher was William P. Vandevert. Bill Vandevert's mother was Grace Clark who was shot and partially scalped in the massacre of the Clark Wagon train near the Snake River in 1851. Her mother was killed in the attack. The remnants of the wagon train made its way west, then camped along the shores of the Deschutes River at what is now Pioneer Park in Bend. Their trip took them on into the Willamette Valley but later, the family returned to the banks of the Deschutes where they established a ranch.

These early ranchers used the open meadows along the river for cattle forage. The meadows, in many cases, were created by the lava flows from Newberry Volcano which blocked the river, forming areas that eventually silted in. The meadows near the planned community of Sunriver* are good examples. The meadows in the Cascade Mountains were also excellent forage in the warm months of the year. In early and late seasons, and in winters, the native bunch grass near Bend sustained cattle with high-protein food. To a great extent, Bend was an area of ranching and grazing until the advent of the timber industry.

Sometime prior to 1903, settlers partially dammed the outlet

---

*Sunriver was built in the late 1960's on the site of a World War II Army Engineering training camp, named for Brig. Gen. Henry Larcom Abbot, who camped there in 1855 as a young Engineer Officer while on the Pacific Railroad Surveys.

of Paulina Lake with a small log dam. This was an attempt to gain water rights and eventually provide irrigation water for ranches in the area west of Newberry Volcano. Today these water rights still exist and the upper 3-feet of Paulina Lake are utilized in this fashion.

On October 5, 1911 the Oregon Trunk Railroad arrived in Bend and its president, James J. Hill, drove the golden spike home. Hill had bested Edward H. Harriman in an expensive and violent race to reach central Oregon via a railroad up the Deschutes Canyon.

At the time of the railroad's arrival, there was an estimated 16-billion board feet of ponderosa pine awaiting. It was said to be the largest remaining stand of pine forests in the West.

Eastern timber barons soon realized the value of these trees and this land. Large timber operators from Minnesota, Michigan, and the southern pine-lands developed an interest in acquiring land under the Timber and Stone Act of 1878. Entrymen falsely filed on claims that were meant to be picked up by homesteaders and ranchers. They could purchase 160 acres of land for $2.50 an acre. Many of these purchasers immediately (and fraudulently) transferred title of the land to others. This scandal reached to the highest levels of government, eventually leading to the removal from office of Oregon's U.S. Senator, John H. Mitchell. This land, which had already been obtained by private interests, was later sold to timber companies and formed the basis for the largest timber operations in the area.

It was about this time that the land currently encompassing Newberry was designated as the Cascade Range Forest Reserve. Land east of the Deschutes River was set aside by President Theodore Roosevelt in July of 1903. The Deschutes National Forest was created out of this preserve on July 1, 1908.

The First World War dramatically increased demand for lumber. In May of that year the Shevlin-Hixon Company of Minnesota announced plans to construct a huge sawmill on the west bank of the Deschutes River. In August, Brooks-Scanlon, also of Minnesota, said they would build an equally large mill on the east side.

Shevlin-Hixon owned more than 200,000 acres of timber. Brooks-Scanlon also owned large tracts. The race as to which firm could cut and mill the most timber was on.

With the impetus of the war, and the need for high production, construction on the mills went rapidly, with the first logs moving through the saws from the ponds in March, 1916. All this activity in the new timber industry brought dramatic growth to Bend. In fact, the town experienced almost a 1,000 percent increase in its population between the years 1910 and 1920.

This period was also during the era of railroad logging. Timber

The "portable" town of Shevlin, including its post office, was moved several times from one forest site to another so its occupants, the workers, would be near logging operations.

operators built and ran their own railroads and both mills at Bend put down rails from their mills into the woods. The mills also purchased standing timber in the National Forest, cut it then train-hauled it to town. Bend became the center of commerce for the mills and for the timbermen's extended operations miles away.

The "town" of Shevlin was really a portable, resident logging camp. While it was complete with bunkhouses and cookhouses, it offered only the spartan living conditions of a forest camp. There were also a few bungalows and square, box-like 1-room shacks said to be quite comfortable.

The timber was cut and moved to the mills on long, slow-moving trains of disconnected trucks and flatcars behind specially built geared locomotives that could negotiate steep and crooked track. The "town" was also moved — even the U.S. Post Office — to a new site. When it was time to go, self-propelled railroad cranes (normally used to hoist overturned locomotives when there were wrecks) moved in, picked up the bungalows and all the shacks with such skill that even a watervase of flowers in water on a table would not spill. These buildings were set on flatcars and down the track they went to the next stand of uncut pine.

The town of Shevlin was known to be in a number of locations including about 10 miles south and between 2 and 3 miles east of Lava Butte, then it was planted about 3 miles southeast of La Pine. Later the "town" was hauled, on newly put-down track, into Klamath County. The portable post office operated from 1931 until spring 1951. The sites of these portable camps are barely visible today and are fading fast, even from the memories of old-timers as they move away or die.

Both Shevlin-Hixon and Brooks-Scanlon placed rails in the area surrounding Newberry Volcano. The early harvests were essentially clear cuts. The timber firms took the valuable ponderosa pine from the lower elevation but stopped when they ascended to the less-marketable lodgepole pine. During this period, these and some smaller firms, took out tens-of-billions of board feet of finished lumber for a nation that was hungry for the forest products.

In 1920 there was a shift in policy — be it ever so slight — when the General Manager of Shevlin-Hixon, from his office in Bend, made a decision. T.J. McCann, the manager, had seen clear-cutting in the middle-west when entire lumber districts had been leveled to where not a single tree was left standing. By direction, he set aside a tract of forest along Tumalo Creek west of Bend. The land, which became Shevlin Park, was deeded to the city on December 22, 1920. It was named for the former president of the company, Thomas H. Shevlin.

In the 1950's, the railroad logging came to a halt throughout most of the Pacific Northwest, as a series of timber-access roads began to penetrate the woods. Harvest continues, although at a much reduced rate, as huge 18-wheel log trucks make their way from yarding areas (loading sites) to the last remaining mill on the east bank of the Deschutes River in the southern end of Bend.

These early ranching, and later timber interests, were the first commercial uses of Newberry Volcano. However, even in the early days, the value of the area for recreation and non-commodity resources was evident.

Perhaps one of the earliest installations was the East Lake Health Resort. This resort was started in 1915 on the southeast shore of the lake and was ready by 1919. The resort was located to take advantage of the hot sulfur springs that bubbled up in the shallow water at the edge of the lake. Oregonians, and people from even farther away, took the primitive road in Model-T Fords to "take the waters" at the resort. The earliest road into the caldera was up the east flank of the volcano.

Old rusting pipes reveal where this water was pumped into the

East Lake Health Resort was on southeast shore of lake. Site today is planted with lodgepole pine.

Guide points to remnant of pipe from East Lake Health Resort. Pipe once carried naturally hot lake water to bathing tubs in resort.

Historical relic: Iron bedrail had been used as reinforcing steel in construction of health resort in 1915.

Public boat launch ramp, southeast area of East Lake, was once part of Health Resort.

White specks in picture are sulphur bubbles coming from bottom of East Lake. This also occurs in Paulina Lake.

resort. There the water filled large wooden tubs in which some vacationers (who believed the waters had restorative powers) would spend many a relaxed hour. The volcanic gases left a distinct sulfur odor about the area. Today, as one walks along the south side of East Lake one can still sniff the fumes which emanate from the lake bed. Small bubbles rise in the shallow water and show volcanic activity. At the right places, one can feel water that is warm to the touch.

Health resorts of this type were common throughout the west and many of them proved to be excellent business ventures. The East Lake Health Resort burned but it was rebuilt. It was open for a few more years when a second fire burned it beyond salvage. This was in 1923.

In time, the Forest Service cleared the area where the buildings had been and planted it in lodgepole pine. All that remains today of the once-thriving resort is an inconspicuous wall of lava rock and the trees.

Fishing is one of the major uses of the National Monument these days. As soon as the snow is gone from the lakes and the high lakes fishing season starts, fishermen can be found in great numbers on both lakes. In late May it can be surprisingly chilly at 6,300-feet with a cool wind blowing. Many is the day that a boat will be launched in snow and snow flurries will fill the air during most of the fishing excursion. The fish are not native to either lake. The early explorers reported only an abundance of crawfish. These apparently ascended to the lakes via Paulina Creek.

Early adventurers noted that the two lakes had an abundance of aquatic life and that they should be good lakes in which to plant fish. About 1910 the first fish were hauled in and planted. James Link, in his book, *Paulina Preferred,* tells the story:

> Early in 1912 a group of men working through the La Pine Commercial Club were bent on stocking these lakes with fish. First we borrowed a fish expert from the Oregon Game Commission to examine the lakes to see if they would sustain fish life. He reported them natural feeding grounds capable of sustaining millions of fish. In July of 1912, the Game Commission shipped us red side fingerlings in 10 gallon cans enough for a four horse wagon load. These arrived one evening in Bend, by this time reached by the new railroad construction, and we were met by our freight outfit. With the road south of Bend in those days merely two ruts with alternating chuckholes every few feet a foot or more deep, it took the outfit all night to make the 62 odd-mile trip to Paulina Prairie, from the east end of which a still rougher road extended up a hogback to the outlet

of Paulina Lake.

At Paulina Prairie our party met the load of fish with fresh draft horses and pack and saddle horses and up the hogback we went some 14 miles. Every few miles we had to climb down into Paulina Creek to carry out buckets of fresh water in order to keep the fish alive. The higher we went, the deeper and rougher the canyon became, but we stayed with it and so finally arrived at the top where we dumped half the fingerlings into Paulina Lake and loaded the other half of the cans into a boat for transportation towards East Lake. It fell my lot to take the pack stock through the brush and over downed trees around the shore of Paulina and to take the fish from there about a mile over to East Lake. We finally dumped the precious cargo into East Lake with no loss worth mentioning.

Another load of fingerlings became available in October that year and were also planted in the lakes. Actively involved with this work were Clyde McKay, a District Game Warden; Paul C. Garrison, a sportsman representing timber interests; and Matt Rychman, superintendent of the State Fish Hatcheries. These fingerlings prospered. A screen was set up to protect the fish from being lost over the falls at Paulina Creek.

The year 1915 saw anglers taking fish weighing as much as 7 pounds. By the 1930's, up to a million fish were being planted in each lake. It remains an excellent fishery to this day with record trout being produced.

Not only is Newberry Caldera a haven for fish, it is also a game sanctuary. Inside the caldera are a variety of animals. In recognition, the State of Oregon declared the area a State Game Refuge. The Forest Service assists the state in preventing hunting in this ecologically important location. The deer, elk, bear, and all waterfowl that dwell there, or migrate through, are protected. During hunting season they can find quiet and rest within the lava flows of the caldera.

Recreationists, hikers, and campers can take comfort in the fact that during hunting season they have no fear from stray bullets. The flanks on the Monument outside the caldera, however, are available for hunting. □

Newberry Left Mark
on Oregon

Professor John Strong Newberry has left his mark on Oregon. The largest volcano in the state is named for this 19th-century physician-naturalist. His ideas on glaciers, mountain ranges, plant geography and erosion were ground-breaking ones. But in spite of this, he seems to be a forgotten man in Oregon history.

Born in Connecticut in 1822, he moved to northern Ohio at an early age. The son of a coal mine owner, Newberry became interested in fossils in his youth. As a teen-ager he became acquainted with Professor James Hall, a prominent geologist, who was also a family friend. Hall was later to assist him in his scientific career.

Newberry graduated from Case Western Reserve University and attended the Cleveland Medical College. He spent two years studying medicine in Paris. After returning to the United States he began medical practice in Ohio, but after five years he apparently decided to change careers.

The United States had become fascinated with the idea of a transcontinental railroad. Congress authorized a series of railroad surveys to be conducted by the Topographical Corps of the Army. These were meant to determine the best route to the West Coast.

It was through his mentor, Professor Hall, that Newberry was named the scientist on the Williamson-Abbot Survey in 1855. This group of the Topographical Corps traveled from the San Francisco Bay area to the Columbia River surveying routes both east and west of the Cascade Mountains. Newberry served as geologist and botanist for the 28-man party.

Oregon was not yet a state and the area was little-known to the rest of the country in any scientific sense. The expedition was a hard and dangerous one. The country that they traveled was unmapped. The co-leader, Lt. Williamson, had seen his own commander, Capt. Warner, killed by Paiute Indians on an 1849 trip in Northern California. Only two years before, Lt. Gunnison had been slain by Indians under similar circumstances. Indeed, a general Indian war broke out during the latter part of the expedition. The party included Lt. Crook and Lt. Sheridan, both of whom went on to later prominence as generals during the Civil War.

The group left the Bay area in May 1855 and entered Oregon south of Klamath Falls in August. They proceeded north along the

Klamath Lake into the upper Deschutes River drainage by September. Along the route the 33-year-old Newberry made many geologic, botanical and zoologic observations.

As the expedition traveled north, they journeyed through the Metolius River area. The first descriptions of Black Butte and the Hoodoos on the Metolius River were from this portion of the survey. The group then traveled to the area of Cove Palisades and on to what is now the Warm Springs Reservation. They crossed the Cascades just south of Mount Hood via a new route. In a little-recognized act of heroism, an Indian youth guided the party over the mountains through a previously untraveled route. This occurred during the middle of an Indian uprising, and he took his life in his hands to accompany the expedition. The party then made its way south through the Willamette Valley [crossing the Umpqua and Rogue Valleys] and returned to the Bay area in January of 1856.

During this expedition Newberry was the first scientist to link the coast ranges of California and Oregon in a geologic and geographic sense. His were the first observations of glacial actions in the Cascade Mountains, and he noted the "drowned forest" in the Columbia River Gorge first seen by Lewis and Clark in 1805-6.

Newberry sent his botanical specimens to Harvard University, where Dr. Asa Gray named Newberry's gentian *(Gentiana newberryi)* and Newberry's figwort *(Penstemon newberryi)* for the explorer. Some consider these to be two of the prettiest wildflowers of the Cascade Range.

Newberry wrote the botanic, geologic and zoologic parts of Volume 6 of the *Pacific Railroad Reports.* The 1855 Williamson-Abbot Survey was part of the final phase of the Pacific Railroad Survey. It strengthened the position of San Francisco as the western terminus for the Transcontinental Railroad.

Two years later Newberry participated in the Ives Expedition. This was partly an effort by the U.S. government to map routes into the Mormon country in preparation for a possible war against Brigham Young.

In 1866 Newberry accepted a full professorship of geology at Columbia University. He helped establish the U.S. Geological Survey. He died in 1892 in New Haven, Connecticut.

Editor's note: This sketch of Dr. Newberry's life appeared under the by-line of Stuart G. Garrett in the *Oregonian* December 25, 1985. Page D-6. □

Jim Teeny brings in another big one from East Lake.

Recreating in the Monument

Hiking and sightseeing are two of the more popular activities in the Monument. Deschutes County Road 21 travels east from Highway 97 and enters the caldera. (Some older maps show Forest Service access road 2120 paralleling the county road but it is no longer passable.) Nice views of Paulina Peak and the surrounding forests can be seen from the county road which has recently been renovated. There are well-maintained and well-marked hiking trails within the Monument and details of these are easily located. Just west of Paulina Lake is the a short trail from an off-road parking lot leading to a spectacular view of Paulina Falls.

Photography is a popular pastime for visitors throughout the Monument. Lava Cast Forest, Lava River Cave, Lava Butte, the Deschutes River and Paulina Peak provide picturesque subjects for family shutterbugs as well as offering challenging scenes for professional photographers. Of particular challenge is making pictures in Lava River Cave which is totally dark except for the glow of rented gasoline lanterns or flashlights.

Winter recreation is an important part of the human side of the Monument. Snowmobiling and skiing are extremely popular activities in the Monument when winter snow levels are adequate. There are a series of trails in the Monument that attract snowmobilers from throughout the Northwest. Paulina Lake Resort welcomes both skiers and snowmobilers through the winter but advance reservations are needed due to limited facilities.

Winter sportsfolk need to be aware that SNO-PARK permits (fee) are *required to be on vehicles before any vehicle can be left unattended in the snow-recreation areas* other than in the franchise areas of the lodge at Paulina Lake. In recent seasons, the highway to the lakes has been blocked with deep snow at the 10-mile SNO-PARK which is 10 miles from Highway 97. East Lake Fishing Resort is closed during winter. Paulina Lake Lodge is open all year but access in winter, with the road closed, is limited to snowmobiles and skiers. The direct route over the snow is the 3-mile run from 10-mile SNO-PARK via the "pole-line" route along the row of power poles to the lodge. The highway is plowed clear of the snow by opening day for high-lake fishing season in mid-May.

Skiers will find a great selection of excellent and exciting trails leading to and within the caldera. Whether the trip be a challeng-

Jordan Mura brought in this 19½ lb., German Brown Trout on a worm. This was on Sept. 1, 1990. East Lake.

ing ski up Paulina Peak or a quiet run on the level, the solitude of Paulina Lake can be rewarding.

Beginning in May, when the high lakes fishing season opens, fishermen are commonly seen on both lakes. Paulina Lake Lodge and East Lake Resort rent boats (and cabins) and the proprietors are friendly and enthusiastic about everyone who visits. They have great advice about:

> What's biting
> What's not biting
> What bait to use
> What bait not to use

One of the world's biggest brown trout was caught here which we will discuss shortly.

East Lake Resort RV Park visitors need to be aware there are no automotive repair or gasoline sales facilities for motor vehicles in the Monument.

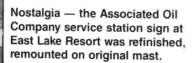

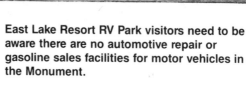

Nostalgia — the Associated Oil Company service station sign at East Lake Resort was refinished, remounted on original mast.

There are four U.S. Forest Service campgrounds within the caldera. Each has adequate facilities and will accept space reservations. Backpacking and camping in undeveloped areas is great sport for those who want to "get away from it all," but one must seek advance information about such outings from Monument personnel regarding seasonal details and fire restrictions.

Lava with lichens (white specks) at base of
Lava Butte.

Jogger near Paulina Lodge.

Sightseeing Trips
Deschutes River

One can visit the scenic area along the Deschutes River at the very northwestern tip of the Monument by turning left as one approaches the Lava Lands Visitor's Center. A 6-mile drive will take you to the end of the road at Benham Falls. Here a small footbridge crosses the river and takes you to a spectacular view of Benham Falls. The large picnic area on the left is the spot where the Brooks-Scanlon Logging Company once held company picnics.

The large ponderosa pines growing here are excellent examples of the early climax pine forests. Fishing is good here. Hiking trails follow the river from here in both directions.

Lava Butte. (Top) Camera faces south. Observe trees grow only on north. (Lower) Camera faces northeast. Line curving around butte is Highway 97. Elevation of the butte is 5,020-feet above sea level.

Trail of the Molten Land, behind Lava Lands Visitor's Center, as viewed from Lava Butte.

Lava Butte Cinder Cone and Lava Flow

Just behind Lava Lands Visitor's Center, is the Trail of the Molten Lava, and the Trail of Whispering Pines. Both of these short foot trails provide close-up views of the amazing natural history of the area.

The Trail of the Molten Lava winds its way across the rough lava flow that was formed when the lava lake in Lava Butte breached and flowed toward the Deschutes River. The Trail of Whispering Pines takes one through a second growth ponderosa pine forest.

Be certain to travel to the top of Lava Butte, elevation 5,020 ft. which is on the red-pavement road and only 1.8 miles from the Lava Lands Visitor's Center. The view from the top is spectacular. On the very top of the butte is a Forest Service Fire Lookout tower which admits visitors a few at a time in summer.

View of limited parking space at summit of Lava Butte. During intense tourist season, Forest Service offers free shuttle from Visitor's center. (Inset) Forest Service fire lookout is at top of butte.

Squirrels atop Lava Butte are a great curiosity to visitors.

Crater atop Lava Butte.

A paved road is available to visitors who wish to drive to the top of Lava Butte. Enter this road from Lava Lands Visitor's Center.

Lava Lands Visitor Center, nestled in the trees, is just off Highway 97 a few miles south of Bend.

Lava Butte on a cold winter day.

Cones from Ponderosa pine trees. These can
usually be seen under the trees near entrance to Lava Lands Visitor's Center.

Forester discusses an exhibit at Lava Lands Visitor Center.

People who are claustrophobic will probably not enjoy a walk underground and even those who claim to enjoy a little spelunking always welcome the sight of daylight which provides a certain sense of relief.

Lava River Cave

Approximately two miles south of the Lava Lands Visitor's Center and on the east side of Highway 97 is the entrance to Lava River Cave. This partially collapsed lava tube is an impressive example of the volcanic geology of central Oregon.

A walk through Lava River Cave with its approximately 40-degree year-around temperature can be welcome relief from outside summer weather often topping 100-degrees.

This is Oregon's longest lava tube. It is about 5,000 feet long and it was formed about 100,000 years ago. Actually, there are two tubes but the tube extending toward the east, about 1,600 feet long, is barricaded to the public due to dangerous conditions. The main tube, which runs toward the west, is near the facility entrance lobby where one is encouraged to rent a lantern. The lanterns are recommended with personal flashlights as backup and to use to point out features within the cave that the general glow of lanterns doesn't pick up. The air in the cave is good and it is cool. One should wear a coat even in summer.

Just before going underground, the descent along the path is within what was, many years ago, part of the lava tube. But the thin

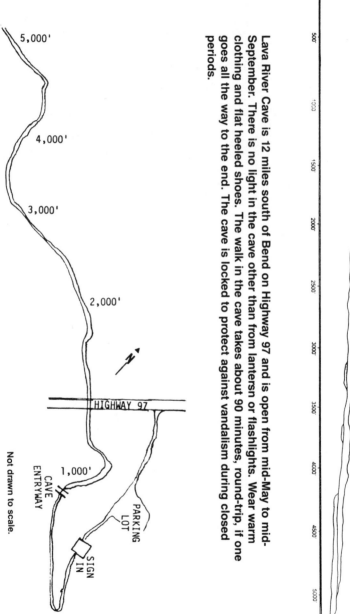

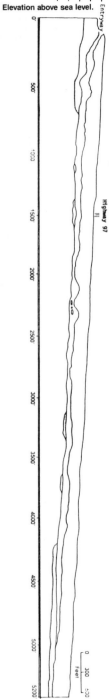

Lava River Cave is 12 miles south of Bend on Highway 97 and is open from mid-May to mid-September. There is no light in the cave other than from lantersn or flashlights. Wear warm clothing and flat heeled shoes. The walk in the cave takes about 90 minutes, round-trip, if one goes all the way to the end. The cave is locked to protect against vandalism during closed periods.

Elevation above sea level.

4500'
4400'
4300'

Entryway

Highway 97

0   300   600
Feet

5,000'

4,000'

3,000'

2,000'

HIGHWAY 97

1,000'

CAVE
ENTRYWAY

PARKING
LOT

SIGN
IN

Not drawn to scale.

84

Old-growth ponderosa pine along path near entrance to Lava River Cave. This area was once part of the lava tube but the roof collapsed leaving this attractive trail.

A single lantern is adequate for a couple of people, but two lanterns allow for better viewing.

Visitors to cave enjoy cool temperature (40°F) as relief from topside often 100° summer heat.

Rod and Cathy Hunt, Santa Rosa, Calif., with 3-month old Jessica (carried), Ryan, 8, sitting on rocks and Randall, 6, with white sweat shirt, pause to enjoy the eerie but fascinating surroundings.

Ponderosa Pine clings to life near Lava River Cave.

roof collapsed and now permits entrance. Like many caves, access here looks little different than any other large hold in the ground.

Just inside the entryway, a metal stairs leads visitors over an area of rock that once fell from the collapsing roof and side walls. These stairs provide access to the tube's main section. On proceeding, note a marker at 1,500 feet where, 80-feet overhead, passes Highway 97.

The area with the highest ceiling, 58-feet, is called "Echo Hall." The ceiling can be viewed if several lanterns are grouped. A little further, tall folks need to mind their heads as the ceiling in "Low Bridge Lane" is limited to 5½ feet. At about 3,200-feet, the cave floor is partially covered with sand. Sand extends to the end of the tube but to reach the very end one must crawl. Lava River Cave is presumed to extend further but a sand plug has not been penetrated.

The environment in the cave is fragile and visitors are encouraged not to disturb or litter or collect samples. Never burn flares or paper. Hibernating bats should never be disturbed. Visitors are urged to use restrooms before entering the cave since it is a long (almost one mile), uphill walk out. □

87

(Top) Ponderosa pine trees, stunted by poor growing conditions, barely survive in Lava Cast Forest. Under ordinary conditions, ponderosa's are 4-times taller. (Lower) Corpse of a tree bleaches in desert dryness and sunlight.

Lone Sentinel. A twisted ponderosa pine. Lava Cast Forest.

Lava Cast Forest

Approximately 9 miles east on Forest Service roads 9720 and 950, from Highway 97, is Lava Cave Forest. This captivating area consists of a series of tree trunk casts formed about 6,000 years ago as fluid lava flowed around the trees then solidified.

Lava Cast Forest is one of the high-interest areas of the Monument but visitors must be advised to carefully attend children, and dogs must be leashed as some of the wells are deep. The access road may be rough depending on time of year and weather but this side trip is worth the effort.

Lava Cast Forest Geological Area

A 1-mile paved trail guides visitors through excellent examples of unique geological formations known as lava casts. These casts, or tree molds, formed about 6,000 years ago as hot lava flowed through a virgin forest covering an area of about 5 square miles on a fault line extending in a westerly direction from Newberry caldera to Lava Butte. As the lava came in contact with the trees,s it solidified around the trunks of the larger trees where it cooled encasing the trees in stone. Many trees burned as the lava engulfed them. Over the centuries, as the remains of the trees disintegrated, only the holes, where the trees once lived — casts — remain.
(Foreground) Paved trail through Lava Cast Forest.

A giant ponderosa once grew here.

Visitors often pose for a snapshot while sitting in one of the holes at Lava Cast Forest.

Paulina Falls in May. For a steady camera position, spread feet, lean elbows on rail, hold your breath and squeeze the shutter button. Margie Webber, photographer, birder and editor, makes photograph appearing on page 35.

Paulina Falls

As one enters the caldera, just to the left is a spectacular view of Paulina Falls. This is the only outlet for surface water from the caldera. The fall of water is about 80 feet around a small island in the center. The rocks in the jumble at the bottom of the falls have broken from the edge of the cliff. Erosion of the face of the falls is gradually closing the distance eastward toward Paulina Lake. One might forecast that the falls will eventually reach the lake then drain the lake!

These specimens of obsidian have been polished for exhibit. Visitors are encouraged to enjoy the flow of obsidian, the lava, and other natural wonders of the Monument which are all called "Oregon Leaverite." ... leave-'er-right where it is so others can enjoy. It is illegal to take any object from the Monument.

Big Obsidian Flow

A recently renovated trail runs out on the forbidding-looking Obsidian Flow. Spectacular formations and flow banding can be seen in the midnight-black chunks of obsidian. The youthfulness and harshness of this environment is demonstrated by the lack of vegetation. An occasional pine tree that has somehow been able to gain a foothold in the lava can be seen. One must bear in mind that this flow is the youngest lava flow in Oregon. At 1,300 years of age, it is in its geologic infancy.

Looking at north face of Paulina Peak.

Paulina Peak

Just before entering the caldera, the road to the right leads to the top of Paulina Peak. This 4+ mile drive is on steep, gravel, one-lane Forest Service access road No. 500 with occasional turnouts. This is rugged travel with views of rugged, beautiful, virgin terrain but it's not a trip for those who require the security of guardrails and don't like heights. Four-wheel drive vehicles, rather than passengers cars, make this trip easier, while small, low-clearance foreign cars should absolutely not be used on this side-trip in the Monument. One should be certain the vehicle has excellent brakes as well as good tires due to risk of tires being cut on rocks. There is no place to pull off to change a tire and there are no telephones for summoning help. But after all this, the view from the summit is spectacular and is undoubtedly the best view anywhere in the state of Oregon. It's a wild, yet peaceful country — the view from the top of Paulina Peak — elevation 7,897 feet.

The view from hiking trail up Paulina Peak is impressive with often the only sound that of the breeze blowing through the trees.

Paulina Peak viewed from Highway 31.

Fort Rock stands lonesome in the desert. (Lower) As viewed from the west.

Outlying Areas

There are a number of side trips that will interest visitors to this unique National Monument. Although these are not within the Monument, they are related.

Fort Rock

Fort Rock State Monument is 38 miles southeast of La Pine, the village on Highway 97 closest to the National Monument. Take Highway 31 to the well-marked junction with a county road, then proceed 7 miles east to the monument. The round trip from La Pine to Fort Rock and back again should take about half-a-day. The highway is good. This trip allows visitors a close look at Oregon's "high desert."

The park area is 190 acres and the supposed fort, remnants of an ancient volcano, is about one-third of a mile across and lies in a crescent shape. Despite its name, there is no evidence it ever served as a "fort." One side of the fort can be entered by car with the high sides as much as 325 feet above the floor of the valley. (A high-clearance vehicle is recommended and make certain the vehicle has good tires.)

Fort Rock is a landmark in the area and is noted for the fact it was near there, in 1938, that Dr. Louis S. Cressman of the University of Oregon, discovered the sandals mentioned earlier.

There is no activity in the park and it is presently unattended, however there are self-guided tours. There is excellent birding in the area. For the history buff with a sense of wonder, a walk through the little cemetery and historical village of Fort Rock (where there is a post office) will be a one-of-a-kind adventure.

Hole-in-the-Ground

The dimensions of this remarkable geologic feature are 450-feet deep and 4,800-feet wide — that's nearly one mile wide.

Although once thought to have been caused by a meteorite impact with the earth, this is a volcanic maar. When the rising magma hit ground water, it spewed rocks up, creating the crater.

An excellent example of forested savannah can be seen from the parking area. As the elevation and precipitation decrease, trees become smaller and farther apart eventually disappearing. The decrease in rain and snow from about 20-inches in the dense pine forest to only about 9-inches at the forest's edge accounts for this slow transition from lush forest to parched sagebrush desert.

To get there, take Highway 31, which runs easterly from Highway 97, about 25 miles to the Forest Service sign indicating road 3125. In a few miles there is a marked turn into road 3130. These roads vary in condition depending on usage and weather and are not high-speed roads at any time. The side trip to the "hole" is worth the effort. Elevation is 4,290 feet.

Big Hole

(NOTE: Hole-in-the-Ground and Big Hole are separate places.)

Another maar, Big Hole was caused by a monumental explosion when raging hot magma collided with underground water. Big Hole is over 6,000-feet in diameter and 425-feet deep. This is located on forest access road #3128 off Highway 31, about 23 miles from La Pine. According to the map, #3128 connects with road #400 which is a circular (loop) road around the bottom of Big Hole. From the road, look up for openings through the trees to see this crater's rim.

A day's excursion might combine visits to Fort Rock, Hole-in-the-Ground and Big Hole on a single trip.

> **Carry food and water especially in hot summer weather.
> These is almost no cellular telephone service in remote areas.**

Dry River Canyon

Highway 20 going east from Bend passes alongside Dry River Canyon for a short distance, starting about 17 miles east of town. It's on the north side of the highway. This is in the Millican Valley but if one sees the highway marker for "Millican" (which was a 1-resident town), you have driven too far.

Dry River is what's left of an ancient river that apparently drained ancient Millican Lake in the High Desert. In some places the canyon is quite deep with the dry river bed in a defile between high basalt walls. The summit on Highway 20 here is 4,304 feet elevation. The view from the summit marker easterly for about 1 mile is great.

Dry River Canyon can be seen east of Bend near
summit marker on Highway 20.

Crack in-the-Ground

Crack-in-the-Ground is probably the weirdest place in Oregon. The "crack" is about 2¾ mile long and 70 feet deep at one point – looks like a skinny roofless cave. Take road to Christmas Valley, look for sign 2 miles east of town: "Crack-in-the-Ground–7 miles." Not recommended for big RV's, 5ᵗʰ wheels. Use BLM lot, walk (wheelchair accessible) about 300 feet to site on rocky path. Spooky and claustrophobic for some, "crack" offers limitless photographic possibilities. Visit with care as this remote eerie phenomena is a highly sensitive biological area.

Lava Island Rock Shelter

For those interested in archaeologic and anthropologic aspects of the Monument, a trip to Lava Island Rock Shelter will head a list of visits one will want to include.

Lava Island Rock Shelter is near the Deschutes River off Century Drive just before reaching the golf course at the Inn of the Seventh Mountain. A short trail leads to this ancient rock shelter where an interpretive sign will be found. There is good hiking along the Deschutes River here with dramatic views of the river's rapids from the trail. □

Newberry's "Big Brown"

This is a fish story. It's a whopper of a fish story. It's a story about the big one that got away - or did it?

The fish was the largest Brown Trout taken in Oregon and when weighed, tipped the scales at 35 pounds, 9 ounces. It was 37 1/2 inches long. It's girth was 26 1/2 inches. *Whoooooooooie!*

Was the catch legal?

Here is Ed Park's story about it:

I am a personal friend of Howard Reed, at the time the owner of Paulina Lake Lodge, who was in on the story.

It was a busy Fourth of July weekend, fishing had been hot, so Howard was busy. There were boats to rent, tackle to sell, questions to answer — the usual activities of a busy lodge and marina.

Therefore Howard wasn't overly impressed when a lady came in about noon with a "big-fish-that-got-away" story. Paulina Lake has produced lots of big fish, and lots of them have gotten away, and Howard, in over forty years of running the lodge, has heard just about everything you can imagine.

Yet something about the lady's story was different, so he did pause a minute to listen. Her story had more than the usual ring of truth to it.

She told of trolling out from the cliffs along the lake's north shore, using a rig commonly used in this country — a multiple-bladed trolling rig and a big night crawler on a single bait hook.

She and her husband had picked up a few nice rainbows, the most common fish in the lake, when she suddenly got a terrific, jolting strike. She set the hook, her husband killed the motor and reeled in his own line, and the fight was on.

The lady was using about 12-pound-test line, so she could put considerable pressure on the fish. Still, as the minutes dragged by, she could not gain any of that line. Instead, the unseen lunker kept taking out line — slowly, stubbornly, steadily.

But it is an open lake, deep, without snags to trouble the angler, and the lady had a big reel full of line. She'd just play him tough and play him out.

The fight went on, the lady grew weary, but apparently the fish didn't. He was still slugging it out with that tough, strong, deep-down fight of a huge brown trout.

Eventually, after over an hour of seesaw fighting, the line went limp, having broken at the knot where it was tied to the string of

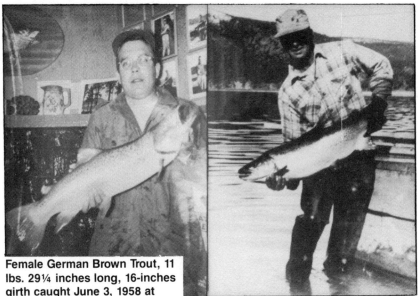

Female German Brown Trout, 11 lbs. 29¼ inches long, 16-inches girth caught June 3, 1958 at East Lake. Ed Coulson, Concord, Calif., was trolling a flatfish on a 4 lb. test line with a 2 lb. test leader.

Arne Shannon with a 30 lb. female German Brown Trout taken during spawning operations at East Lake in November 1952.

spinners. The lady's fight was over, and all she had to show for it was the memory of playing a really tremendous trout. Unfortunately, Howard did not get her name, and to this day we have not been able to track down her identity.

But the mighty brown trout's fight was not over. He still had that annoying string of spinners and line in his jaw, and he was considerably weakened by the hour-long struggle against the whip of the fiberglass rod. His strength was gone. He needed rest, badly.

And so the giant Paulina Lake brown eventually came to the surface to lie on its side, spent, with gill covers barely working. Life no longer was a certain thing. The struggle had been too great.

That afternoon another pair of anglers were trolling about 100 feet out from Paulina's east shore. Ira Fox and his son, Darrell, of Eugene, Oregon, were also catching some pretty nice rainbows. It was a good day, and father and son were enjoying the outing.

I've talked with Mr. Fox and he filled me in on the details:

> On one swing heading southward this object surfaced 50 or 60 feet in front of us, I figured at first it was a chunk of log. It being a fish never entered my head because of its size. When we got a little closer Darrell says, 'It's a dead fish!' So I eased

The beach at East Lake Resort. Paulina Peak.

Fishing in early spring on East Lake still partially
covered with snow-topped ice. Central Pumice Cone in
background. Area of lake in front of what's called the
White Slide, on the cone, is termed one of the best
fishing holes.

Dozens of boats take to the lakes. Most are occupied by fishermen.

up close to get an idea how really big it was. Then Darrell says, 'It's got a lure in its mouth,' and with the price of fishing gear, I decided we should get it. So Darrell reached and got hold of the spinners. The tug caused the fish to sluggishly dive down aways, then it came back to the surface. This is when we realized it was not dead. I told Darrell to grab the front end of him, being careful not to get bitten, and I'd try to get the net over the back half.

In this manner we wrestled it into the boat and this is where the real battle took place as the fish suddenly decided it didn't like its surroundings, and really started to flip around. It almost got Darrell flipped overboard trying to wrestle it into submission. Finally with one of the oars Darrell was able to hit it on the head enough to quiet it.

Of course when Mr. Fox and his son brought that huge fish to the lodge, Howard Reed was astounded. Immediately he remembered the story the lady had told him earlier that day. He tried to locate the woman but was unable to do so. She'll probably never know that she came awfully close to setting a new North American record for brown trout.

This Paulina Lake brown was also inspected by the Oregon Game Commission, officially weighed and measured and examin-

Cabin at East Lake Resort.

Area of trees (center) was site of early day health resort.
Photographed in May 1991.

Historic boat-roller exhibited at East Lake Resort. This was the easy way to up-end a boat for repairs, painting.

ed. Ira Fox took the fish home to Eugene, not really sure of what to do with it. Since he himself didn't legally catch it, he wasn't too excited about having it mounted.

But a friend, Gary Poissant, took the fish to have it mounted, offering to pay for it himself, since he realized the significance of the fish's size. After the fish was mounted it was given to Gary's father, who managed a hardware store in the nearby town of Corvallis.

The fish was in Corvallis for a couple years before I was able to run it down, buy it from the owner, and return it to central Oregon. I have no claim whatsoever on the fish, except that I own it, but it certainly does make an interesting conversation piece — the second largest brown trout ever reported from North America and the third largest in the world.

Paulina Lake's big brown was landed July 3, 1965. A brown caught in Utah was 36 pounds 12 ounces, 36 1¾2 inches long, 28-inch girth. A brown caught in Scotland holds the world's record at 39 1/2 pounds. But the Utah and the Paulina Lake brown trout, as beautiful a record as each angler can hope for, were declared illegal by fish and game people.

The "big brown," as it's called, is presently on exhibit at Mountain Country Sporting Goods in Bend. □

Dads fish, moms visit, knit, read, while kids play in snow in May. East Lake Resort.

Two-family camper-fishermen at East Lake, pose for snapshot before going home. Although lake was still about half iced-in, opening day fishing in May always brings out a crowd.

(Top) Cabin at Paulina Lake Lodge. (Lower) The lodge restaurant.

Paulina Lake with thawed area in February. Camera faces northeast.

Paulina Lake looking northeast from Paulina Creek
Bridge. May 1991.

Lower end of Paulina Lake has grassy, swamp area
known for mosquitoes.

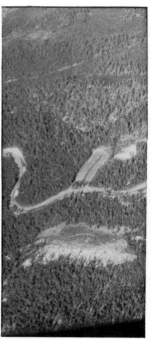

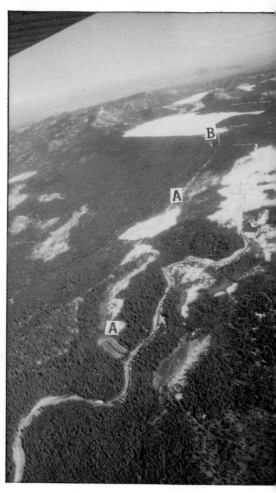

(Left photo) Ribbon like line through center of view is access road to lakes from Highway 97. U-shaped clear area is 10-MILE SNO-PARK (fee parking lot in winter). Road east of sno-park is usually blocked with deep snow and road is closed with locked gate. (Right) View facing easterly. SNO-PARK on left at (A). In winter, snowmobilers follow 3-mile "pole-line" trail (A) to Paulina Lake Lodge (B).

Snowmobiles along pole line trail. (Center) — at Paulina Lake Lodge. (Lower) — at East Lake Resort.

Paulina Lodge in winter dress greets snowmobilers and skiiers.

Geothermal Resources of the Newberry Area

Newberry is considered one of the top geothermal energy sources in the Pacific Northwest. The recent volcanic activity at Newberry indicates there is probably a shallow magma body below the volcano. Geologic evidence suggests a body (or bodies) from two to five kilometers deep which may range from small basaltic intrusions to larger magma chambers with silicic tops. This magma would be the source of the numerous recent volcanic eruptions over the last few thousand years at Newberry. This body or bodies would also be responsible for the hot springs and fumaroles that still are present within the caldera.

Estimates by the Bonneville Power Administration have ranged up to 1,500 megawatts for the energy production potential. To fully exploit this type of resource could require 30 geothermal plants of 50 megawatts each.

Geothermally produced electricity offers some advantages over

"The Dome" southeast of East Lake.

nuclear and fossil-fuel types of production. It avoids the impact on fisheries that dams create. If properly utilized, it is a safe energy source. It incurs few of the long-term waste disposal problems of nuclear energy. It does not contribute significantly to global-warming, as fossil fuel burning does. However, care must be taken in the development of geothermal energy in order to minimize potential impacts on the environment. A geothermal plant is a large industrial facility and in the wrong place could adversely affect a variety of natural values. Care and sensitivity will be shown in the development of any geothermal power at Newberry.

In 1989, the BLM and the Forest Service issued a permit for a test production well to be drilled on the west flank of Newberry Volcano outside the National Monument boundary. Due to economic difficulties, the firm holding the permit for this project has been unable to drill this well as of spring 1991. The predicted energy shortage in the Pacific Northwest will place added importance on renewable sources of electrical energy such as those found at Newberry Volcano. □

East Lake sunset.

About the Author

Stuart G. Garrett is a medical doctor with a strong interest in history and natural history. He lives in Bend with his daughter, Ragan. He has practiced family medicine in Bend since 1978. He served as President of the Native Plant Society of Oregon, co-founded the High Desert Chapter of NPSO, served on the board of the Oregon Chapter of the Nature Conservancy, and chaired the Newberry Volcano National Monument Committee which success-fully sought national monument designation at the volcano.

Bibliography

Aikens, Melvin. *Archaeology of Oregon*. U.S. Dept. of Interior — BLM. 1984.

Arno, Stephen and Ramona Hammerly. *Northwest Trees*. Mountaineers. 1977.

Broghan, Phil. *East of the Cascades*. Binford & Mort. 1964.

Couture, Marilyn. *Recent and contemporary foraging practices of the Harney Valley Paiute*. Unpub. M.A. thesis, Department of Anthropology, Portland State University. 1978.

Cressman, Luther S. *The Sandal and the Cave*. Oregon State Univ. Pr. 1981.

Crittenden, Mabel and Dorothy Telfer. *Wildflowers of the West*. Celestial Arts. 1975.

Eliot, Willard A. *Birds of the Pacific Coast*. Putnam. 1923.

Fremont, John C. *Report of the Exploring Expedition to the Rocky Mountains and to Oregon and North California*. (U.S. Government Washington, D.C.) 1845.

Geology and Mineral Resources of Deschutes County, Oregon. Oregon Department of Geology and Mineral Industries Bulletin No. 89. 1976.

Goetzmann, William. *Exploration and Empire*. Knopf. 1966.

————————————— . *New Lands, New Men*. Viking. 1986.

Hatton, Raymond L. *High County of Central Oregon*. Binford & Mort. 1980.

Helbock, Richard W. *Oregon Post Offices 1847-1982*. La Posta. 1982.

Higgins, Michael W. and Aaron D. Waters. "Newberry Caldera Field Trip," in *Andesite Conference Guidebook*, Oreg. State Dept. Geology & Mineral Industries, Bulletin 62. 1968.

Hitchcock, C. Leo *et al*. *Vascular Plants of Pacific Northwest; (Vol. I) Vascular Cryptograms, Gymnosperms & Monocotyledons*. Univ. of Wash. Press. 1969.

Jensen, Robert A. *Roadside Guide to the Geology of Newberry Volcano*. CENOREGEOPUB (Bend). 1988.

Minor, Rick and Katheryn Toepel. *Lava Island Rock Shelter and Early Hunting Camp in Central Oregon*. Idaho Museum of Natural History No. 34. Idaho State University Press. 1984.

Linck, James. *Paulina Preferred*. Binford & Mort. 1945.

McArthur, Lewis A. *Oregon Geographic Names*. Fifth Edition. Oregon Historical Society Press. 1982.

Ogden, Peter Skene. *Snake Country Journal 1826-27*. K.G. Davies, Editor. - Hudson's Bay Record Society (London). 1961.

Peterson, Roger T. *Field Guide to Western Birds*. Houghton/Mifflin. 1990.

Puter, Stephen A.D. *Looters of the Public Domain*. Arno. 1972.

Russell Israel C. *Preliminary Report on the Geology and Water Resources of Central Oregon*. U.S. Government Printing Office. 1905.

Webber, Bert & Margie. *Railroading in Southern Oregon and the Founding of Medford*. YeGalleon. 1985.

Zucker, Jeff, Kay Hummell & Bob Hogfoss. *Oregon Indians*. Oregon Historical Society Press. 1983.

Illustration Credits

Trail of the Molten Land starts at Lava Lands Visitor's Center.

Index

Photographs are shown in *italic*

First "official" sign designating the Monument placed over earlier sign on Dedication Day, June 30, 1991.

Meeting between Stu Garrett, Dave McClain, Rep. Bob Smith, Tom Throop, John Grant in Washington D.C. in June 1990 at Monument hearing before Congress.

Dedication Day, June 30, 1991. Activities and entertainment for visitors of all ages at Ogden Group Camp, Newberry National Volcanic Monument.

The U.S. Postal Service temporary post office at Ogden Campground serviced covers by imprinting special postmark available only on June 30, 1991. The long line awaits this service. For the postmark see page 15.

Paulina Lake   Central Pumice Cone   East Lake

Paulina Peak

— Original China Painting
by Beverly Jungwirth

Notes